KEEPING IT REAL

WHAT IT WILL TAKE TO FOLLOW JESUS

WESLEY PENNINGTON

Keeping It Real
by Wesley Pennington

ISBN 978-1-63360-353-0

For Worldwide Distribution
Printed in the USA

Urban Press
PO Box 5044
Williamsburg, VA 23188
757.808.5776
www.urbanpress.us

ACKNOWLEDGMENT

I would like to thank my wife, Marissa. for always supporting me in the ministry, for being by my side through everything and following me even when she wasn't sure. I would also like to thank my two daughters, Ashley and Eliana, for helping me to see and feel the love of Christ. Through you I have learned how our Heavenly Father sees and feels for us His children.

I would also like to thank my Rally Point Saturday morning men's group. My brothers, you have challenged and sharpened me. I am grateful.

Last but certainly not least I would like to thank You, Lord, for calling me and never doubting me. Your love has drawn me deep into Your heart. I love You, Lord!

www.ingramcontent.com/pod-product-compliance
Lightning Source LLC
La Vergne TN
LVHW091634100826
845152LV00002B/32

FOREWORD VII
INTRODUCTION XI

CHAPTER 1
HOW DO MEN COMMIT? 1

CHAPTER 2
WHAT IT LOOKS LIKE WHEN MEN COMMIT 14

CHAPTER 3
GOD'S COMMITMENT TO US 26

CHAPTER 4
THE CALL TO COMMIT 38

CHAPTER 5
THE CHOICE TO FOLLOW JESUS 49

CHAPTER 6
THE DIFFERENCE BETWEEN
KNOWING AND FOLLOWING 61

CHAPTER 7
THE RESULT OF KNOWING JESUS 74

CHAPTER 8
WHAT DOES SURRENDER LOOK LIKE? 92

CHAPTER 9
SHOWING UP! 108

CHAPTER 10
LET YOUR YES BE YES! 121

CHAPTER 11
CAN WE KEEP IT REAL? 135

CHAPTER 12
CONCLUSION AND FINAL THOUGHTS 155

ABOUT THE AUTHOR

FOREWORD

I met Wesley Pennington in 2021, and since then I've had the privilege of knowing him not only as an author, pastor, colleague, and friend, but as a man. I've spoken in his church, worked closely with him in editing and publishing his books, and watched his life up close. That matters, because in a book like this the message only carries weight if the messenger lives what he teaches. Wes does.

In publishing, I've learned that credibility isn't established by good writing alone. It's established by integrity. Many people can write about commitment, surrender, and following Jesus. Far fewer can speak about those things with moral authority. Wes can, however, because what you're about to read isn't theory. It's testimony. He has walked the road he invites you to walk. He has faced failure, wrestled with fear, learned obedience, and allowed God to reshape his heart. And he continues to do that work today.

I'm intimately acquainted with Wes' material and I can say without hesitation that he is the same man on the page that he is in person. He doesn't pretend. He doesn't exaggerate. He doesn't hide behind religious language. He tells the truth about himself so others can find the truth about God. That kind of honesty is rare, and it's exactly what makes this book so important.

Keeping It Real isn't a comfortable read. It's not meant to be. Wes is writing to men who want and need more than shallow faith and convenient Christianity. He's writing to men who need to know there is more to following Jesus than church attendance and good intentions. With clarity and compassion, he draws a sharp line between knowing about Jesus and actually knowing Him. He reminds us that discipleship always costs something, and that real faith always shows itself in obedience, surrender, and love.

What impresses me most about Wes is that he teaches what he practices. I've seen his commitment to his family, his church, and the men God has entrusted to him. I've seen him walk with men patiently, pray with them, challenge them, and refuse to give up on them when their faith wavers. That's why his words ring true. He's not offering advice from a distance; he's inviting you into a life he himself is pursuing.

If you're willing to be honest with yourself, this book can change you. It will confront you, encourage you, and call you to rise up and go higher. More importantly, it will point you toward the kind of relationship with Jesus that transforms not only your beliefs, but your character, your relationships, and your purpose.

I'm grateful to call Wes a friend, an author, and a fellow servant of Christ. I'm even more grateful that you are about to hear his voice.

Dr. John W. Stanko
Urban Press

PREFACE

Let me start with a word about the author, Wes Pennington, who lives the words of this book. He is a Christ follower, pastor, and community leader. His words in this book have been road tested in the daily life of this humble and godly man.

There is a difference between saying something is real and living as if it is. This book, *Keeping It Real*, is a road map to help us connect our words to our actions, to make our walk resemble our talk.

We live in a time when words are cheap, commitments are flexible, and devotion is often reduced to feelings or moments of inspiration. Yet deep inside every man is a quiet awareness that we were made for more – more than drifting, more than distraction, more than surface-level belief. We were made for a life anchored in something unshakable. We were made for a life fully given to Jesus Christ.

Keeping It Real is about that kind of life.

At the center of this book is a simple but life-altering premise: *real life begins with real commitment to Jesus.* Not a partial commitment. Not a convenient commitment. But a wholehearted, surrendered, enduring "yes" to the Son of God who first said "yes" to us.

Before this book ever asks what commitment looks like from us, it begins where Scripture begins—with God's commitment to us. The story of our faith does not start with our pursuit of Him, but with His relentless pursuit of us. When we were distant, He came near. When we were unfaithful, He remained faithful. When we were not committed to Him, Jesus was fully committed to us—all the way to Gethsemane, all the way to the cross. Calvary is the ultimate declaration that God does not love halfway.

That truth changes everything.

Because when a man sees the depth of God's commitment, his own walls begin to come down. The guarded heart softens. Excuses lose their power. Faith becomes more than agreement with ideas; it becomes a response of love. Commitment is no longer driven by guilt or pressure, but by gratitude and awe.

From there, the question becomes unavoidable: *What does a committed life actually look like?*

It looks like a character that gets us out of bed, commitment that moves us into action, and discipline that helps us follow through. It looks like a heart wholly true to the Lord. It looks like a man who allows God to shape his inner life, not just his public image. It looks like surrender that echoes Jesus' prayer in the garden: "Not my will, but Yours be done."

This book draws a clear line between merely *knowing about* Jesus and truly *following* Him. Following Jesus is not like following a team, a trend, or a favorite voice. It is not admiration from a distance. It is a daily decision to deny ourselves, take up our cross, and walk in step with Him. It is a reordering of life where Christ, not self, stands at the center.

And yet, this life of surrender is not heavy with despair—it is filled with grace. To be fully known and truly loved by God frees a man from pretending. It humbles his pride, steadies him in difficulty, and gives him courage to live honestly before God and others. His grace is not theory; it is power for real life.

Commitment then moves from the abstract to the everyday. It shows up in faithfulness—in marriage, in fatherhood, in church, in work, in community. It shows up in being present, in keeping our word, in letting our "yes" truly be yes. It shows up in the unseen places of the heart, where motives are examined and authenticity replaces performance. We may fool others. We may even fool ourselves. But Jesus sees what is real—and invites us into a life where we no longer have to hide.

Keeping It Real is a call—not to perfection, but to sincerity. Not to image management, but to integrity. Not to casual Christianity, but to courageous, wholehearted devotion.

In the end, this book is an invitation to men:

to step up,
to lay down their lives,
to love God deeply,
and to follow Jesus fully.

Because when our commitment to Him becomes real, everything else in life begins to fall into its proper place.

Enjoy the journey.
Nick Fatato
Network Superintendent
Southern New England Ministry Network

INTRODUCTION

Anyone who does not love does not know God, because God is love.
– 1 John 4:8

"We have to recognize that there cannot be relationships unless there is commitment,
unless there is loyalty, unless there is love,
patience, persistence."
– Cornel West

This is a book about something I have found many men struggle with. I know for much of my life, the word commitment was a negative word. I did not like it nor did I choose to abide by it. I was committed to my football and basketball teams, but it was a totally different situation when it came to people. For me, commitment with other men always had to do with us competing together (nothing more). But when it came to women, I was afraid of giving up some part of me to them that I may never be able to get back.

If you have heard me speak or have read my other books, you know I am going to be truthful about myself. The truth is important because I want you to know that the person who wrote this book understands your struggle. Believe me that when it comes to the concept of commitment, I know your struggle.

The passage I quoted at the beginning says that anyone who does not love does not know God, because God is love. That is a significant truth to digest. The reason I say that is because when we mistreat others because we cannot keep a commitment we have made, when we go back on our word, it shows a lack of love. If we are lacking love, then we do not know God.

That's painful for me to say and admit because I have always thought I loved God. Truthfully, I was saying I did not love God by not making or keeping commitments because love is not afraid to commit. Love keeps its word, and love respects.

I can honestly say that in my past relationships, even though I thought I loved, I really did not show love. Because I did not love even though I called myself a Christian, God was not in me. Saying that makes me sad, but God convicted me that this is the truth. So when I say I understand your struggle, I really do.

So what is the point of this book? It is to understand why commitment is so important to God. The word commitment is used 164 times in the Bible from Genesis to Revelation. Because commitment is mentioned so often in the Bible indicates it must represent something important to God. For us to really be the men of

God we are called to be, we will need to be able to commit.

Cornel West said there cannot be relationship if there is no commitment. I believe this is why it is so important to God. If we cannot commit to the people in our lives, we cannot commit to God because we have no love. If we have no love, we cannot know God.

God wants to have a relationship with us. Maybe that is why so many men struggle in our relationship with God. If we struggle with commitment, we will struggle building a meaningful relationship with God. As I write this, I understand that my struggles with following God in my life were due to my struggle with commitment. Commitment, or the lack thereof, has implications for many things in our lives—family, work, ministry, and our growth in the Lord.

I retired as a Rhode Island **State Trooper** in 2023. Many of my struggles during my time as a trooper occurred because I was not as committed as I should have been. My supervisors saw my lack of commitment, and it affected my standing at work. I learned firsthand that a lack of commitment can affect my employment, making me less desirable for promotions and more meaningful work. It was not until I was able to commit to being a good trooper that my career turned around. In fact, it was not until I committed to God that I was able to commit to the job. But I am getting ahead of myself here. My point is that we as men often struggle with commitment.

I caused a lot of heartache simply because of my stubborn resistance to commit. A girl who fell in love with me had no chance of it turning into a relationship. The moment the relationship became too serious, I was looking for a way to get out of it. The reason I would look for a way out was because I was afraid to commit. If I am totally transparent with you (and I want to be), I always felt like there was something I would be missing if I made a commitment. I thought that there was something more or better ahead so I resisted. I kept my options open. It was always all about me.

What's more, I was afraid. I did not want to work on anything that would require me being exposed in any way, especially if it meant sharing the inner most things of my heart. I have found through being a men's pastor that many men have this same sentiment. We feel that way because when we were little boys, we were told to be hard and not to cry. We were told not to let others see they had hurt us. It's the same principle as the saying which says, "Don't let them see you sweat." I was an expert at not letting them see me sweat.

So, if your one of the women I dated in my past, I want to say I am sorry. You just met me at the wrong time. God had not yet taken over my heart. I can say now I have learned commitment and through this book I am going to tell you how and why. I hope that by the end you will be encouraged to not be afraid to commit. Remember that relationship means commitment and God wants a relationship. And I have made a lifetime commitment to my wife and daughters and of course to the Lord Jesus Christ.

A little further down from the passage I quoted says,

> If anyone says, "I love God," and hates his brother, he is a liar; for he who does not love his brother whom he has seen cannot love God whom he has not seen. And this commandment we have from him: whoever loves God must also love his brother (1 John 4:20-21).

There are different forms of hate. When we think of hate, we usually think of it in terms of an intense feeling or negative emotion. Hate is the opposite of love. We think we can be indifferent but in God's eyes that is the same as hate. So, when we treat each other in an indifferent way, what we are really saying is that we hate them. If we do that, then the word of God says we are liars if we say we love Him.

I know that I am **giving** a narrow interpretation of the Word, but Jesus always wants to take us deeper. Here I am saying that indifference is the same as hate. For example, if I can help someone and I refuse to do so, is that love? And if the other person will suffer or lack because of my indifference, isn't that the same result as if I hated them because I did not want what was in their best interests? Would a person who hated someone hold back anything that would benefit the one they hated? Of course they would. Then what's the difference between me being indifferent or hating? In the end, I have chosen not to help someone I could have helped. God wants us to love one another, and commitment shows our love that we have if for no one else than God.

In the next chapter, I will talk about how we as men commit. Let's talk about commitment but not just to talk about it, but to learn how to do it as God would have us do.

"The truest form of love is how you behave toward someone, not how you feel about them."
– Steve Hal

REFLECTION QUESTIONS

1. Have you struggled with commitment? When? How? How did you behave? Why were you so noncommittal?
2. How would your past relationships say you were in regards to commitment?
3. What would God say about your commitment?

CHAPTER 1

HOW DO MEN COMMIT?

"To be loved but not known is comforting but superficial. To be known and not loved is our greatest fear. But to be fully known and truly loved is, well, a lot like being loved by God. It is what we need more than anything. It liberates us from pretense, humbles us out of our self-righteousness, and fortifies us for any difficulty life can throw at us."
– Timothy Keller

"If a man vows a vow to the Lord or swears an oath to bind himself by a pledge, he shall not break his word. He shall do according to all that proceeds out of his mouth."
– Numbers 30:2

The verse from Numbers should convict most of us. I think about how many vows I have made and did not keep—including the vows I made in my first marriage. I was not committed in the way I should have been, and it cost me that marriage. It cost me not being in the life of my oldest daughter and missing so many important moments in her life. A lack of commitment can truly steal some very important moments in your life.

So, the question that begs to be asked is how do we as men commit. How can we commit in a way that we keep our word and follow through on what we say? This for us is impossible because we do not have the ability on our own to honor such things. If we take the time to think about it, this is a bit crazy. The reason I say that is because most little boys grow up wanting to be a knight in shining armor for someone—usually a young lady.

This is the oath of a knight of King Arthur's Round Table and we should all take it to heart.

> I will develop my life for the greater good. *I will place character above riches*, and *concern for others above personal wealth.* I will never boast, but cherish humility instead. *I will speak the truth at all times, and forever keep my word.* I will defend those who cannot defend themselves. I will honor and respect women, I will uphold justice by being fair to all. *I will be faithful in love and loyal in friendship,* I will abhor scandals and gossip—neither partaking nor delighting in them. I will be generous to the poor and to those who need help. I will forgive when asked that my own

mistakes will be forgiven. I will live my life with courtesy and honor from this day forward.

This may not represent the exact words that a knight would say, but it serves the purpose of my point. This is what many of us dreamed about when we were little ones. It was a lofty ideal but one that we could never live up to. The problem is that we have a sin tendency that Jesus needs to deal with. We have to allow Him to change us. If we do not allow that to happen, we will continue to live with our sin problem. I will talk more about this later. For now, let's just say that on our own, we could not be the men that as little boys we wished we could be. This is painful to face but at the same time it's life-changing. If I cannot do it on my own, it means there must be a Savior who can help me with this.

Like I mentioned in the Introduction, it was not until I started to be a son of God that I learned about commitment and received the power to carry it out. It was not something I figured out; it was something I observed. You see, once I became a son of God, I observed His commitment to me. Every time I did not show Him love by my actions, He still loved me. Every time I lied to someone (and I am sorry I did), God still loved me. Every time I did my own thing instead of following through on my word, God still loved me. God stands behind His word because His word says that He neither leaves nor forsakes me.

> Hebrews 13:5-6 states, "Keep your life free from love of money, and be content with what you have, for he has said, 'I will never leave you nor forsake you.' So we can confidently say, 'The Lord is my helper; I will not fear; what can man do to me?'"

> Deuteronomy 31:6-8 says, "Be strong and courageous. Do not fear or be in dread of them, for it is the Lord your God who goes with you. He will not leave you or forsake you." Then Moses summoned Joshua and said to him in the sight of all Israel, "Be strong and courageous, for you shall go with this people into the land that the Lord has sworn to their fathers to give them, and you shall put them in possession of it. It is the Lord who goes before you. He will be with you; he will not leave you or forsake you. Do not fear or be dismayed."

The same thing God said in Hebrews and Deuteronomy He is saying to us now: He will never leave us nor forsake us. What a powerful example of commitment that we can see in our Father God. And let's not forget about Jesus and what He did on the cross. That took extreme commitment to His purpose and to His

Father. We can learn what commitment looks like through our Lord and Savior's example. He is committed to His Father and He is committed to us. We just have to have eyes to see and ears to hear what the Lord is saying and doing.

I have shared this before but it is worth sharing again. When I was at my worst, it was then that the Holy Spirit told me He never doubted me. It was not when I became Pastor Wes, it was when I was at my worst. If that does not show commitment, I don't what does. It blows my mind that when I was not committed to anyone, my Lord was committed to me. That deserves a moment to pause and reflect.

So, for us to get an understanding of what commitment looks like, all we have to do is look to Jesus. We see so many passages showing His commitment. The commitment to go where the Father sends Him. The commitment to say what the Father tells Him to say. The commitment to endure whatever He has to in order to obey the Father.

As we look at Jesus, we see that commitment takes courage. I would have said throughout my life that I had courage, but the truth is that I did not. Jesus showed courage and He was strong in the face of adversity and in the light of others rejecting and persecuting Him. Through it all, He still kept His word and followed through. The only way we can learn to commit is to allow ourselves to be transformed into the image of Jesus. This image was the image that was spoken about in Genesis 1:26-27:

> Then God said, "Let us make man in our image, after our likeness. And let them have dominion over the fish of the sea and over the birds of the heavens and over the livestock and over all the earth and over every creeping thing that creeps on the earth." So God created man in his own image, in the image of God, he created him; male and female he created them.

This is the image God made at the beginning and the image that was distorted when sin came into the world. This is the same image that Jesus is restoring as He transforms us in the power of the Spirit. Man was made in His image and now that the curse of sin has been broken Jesus is transforming us back into the image we were supposed to have–into His image, the likeness of one who keeps His word and honors His Father.

For us to learn how to be committed, we must allow Jesus to transform us back into the original image that we were made in. Only then will we have a chance to be committed men. Of course, we have free will so we can refuse to cooperate with this, but if we truly love God, then we must let love change us, and let love show us commitment. The relationship that I am referring to is all about commitment.

When I realized that God was committed to me, I started to understand what He wanted to do in me. I allowed Him to change me and in the changing I learned how to be more committed as a man. I have to say that I am still a work in progress and my Lord and Savior is still showing me new levels of commitment. But I am far from where I was then, and now I can look back and see all the damage I caused because of my lack of commitment.

We first must learn to commit to God before we can ever think of committing to anyone else. The only way we can learn that is if we can see the extent to which He has committed Himself to us. I have said it before and I will say it again: Jesus is the linchpin of our salvation and freedom, which includes commitment.

I never thought that I would be freer when I learned commitment than when I was not committed to anything. I thought that by not committing to anything I was free. I am freer now than ever before and that is because Jesus Christ has set me free from the stronghold of being double-minded and hesitant to commit to someone or something.

When we learn commitment, we learn integrity. Our character is then formed in the forges of God's fire. We go in as a poor example of masculinity, and we come out strong and purified as gold. This is the work of God in our lives. We have to be willing to let Him change us into the image of Jesus Christ. That truth is powerful and life changing.

This is the way we become men of integrity and are able to commit to those we love. This is how we become committed husbands. This is how we become committed fathers, and this is how we become committed men of God.

LET'S PRAY:

Father in Heaven I come before You a mess and lacking in so many areas. I know that only You can transform me into the image you first created us to be. I'm putting my life in Your hands. Transform and change me into whatever You want me to be. I will go where You tell me to go and say what You tell me to say. I'm committed to You in every way. Keep my heart soft and my mind focused on Your plan and purpose in my life. Teach me commitment, Lord, and create in me a steadfast heart. Make me a man of integrity in Jesus' name I pray, amen!

SUMMARY POINTS

1. I cannot commit in my own strength; commitment begins with transformation by Christ.
2. God's commitment to me becomes the standard for my commitment to others.
3. Integrity is revealed by whether I keep my word when it costs me something.
4. True commitment restores the image of God in a man's life.

BIBLE VERSES USED IN THIS CHAPTER:

Number 30:2
Hebrews 13:5-6
Deuteronomy 31:6-8
Genesis 1:26-27

REFLECTION QUESTIONS

1. Where in your life have you lacked commitment?
2. How does your version of commitment look when compared to God's?
3. How can you learn to be more committed?
4. How does your commitment to God translate to your family and friends?
5. What is your next step to become more committed?

ADDITIONAL STUDY

If we are going to keep it real, most of us struggle with commitment long before we struggle with obedience. The problem isn't that we don't know what to do—it's that we don't trust God enough to surrender control. Commitment exposes our fear of loss, our desire to protect ourselves, and our tendency to rely on our own strength.

Jesus is not asking us to try harder. He is asking us to be honest. He knows that apart from Him, we cannot keep our word, stand firm under pressure, or follow through when commitment costs us something. That is why commitment is not a matter of willpower—it is a matter of transformation. Before we ask whether we can commit, we must ask whether we are willing to let God change us.

1.
JOSHUA'S COVENANT DECISION
JOSHUA 24:14-24

Joshua forced the people to confront reality. He told them to stop pretending and choose whom they would truly serve. Commitment begins when excuses end and allegiance becomes clear.

2.
ABRAHAM'S OBEDIENCE
GENESIS 22:1-14

God was never testing Abraham's love for Isaac—He was revealing Abraham's trust in God. Commitment is exposed when obedience requires us to release what we hold most tightly.

3.
PSALM 15

This psalm describes the man who keeps his word even when it hurts. That kind of integrity cannot be faked. It flows from a heart anchored in God, not self-preservation

CHAPTER 2

WHAT IT LOOKS LIKE WHEN MEN COMMIT

It was character that got us out of bed, commitment that moved us into action, and discipline that enabled us to follow through.
- Zig Ziglar

"Let your heart therefore be wholly true to the Lord our God, walking in his statutes and keeping his commandments, as at this day."
- 1 Kings 8:61

It is amazing that when I was a young man, commitment was difficult for me to understand. I did not like it nor was I prepared to give it. I had a hard time giving my heart to anyone. There was a wall around it that was unbreakable, at least by human means. The only one who could break my walls down was Jesus Christ. Once I decided to accept Him as my Lord and Savior, my life changed.

I saw Jesus who was committed to me even when I at times was not committed to Him. As

I started to observe His commitment to me, I started to compare His commitment to my own. I was truly found wanting in the area of commitment. Jesus is a great model of commitment. Think about it for a second. In order to go to the cross and pay the price He paid for us, He had to be totally committed. The Word says He "set His face" when it was time to go to Jerusalem for His execution (see Luke 9:51).

As a trooper for the Rhode Island State Police, I once had to respond to someone who jumped off a bridge in one of our communities. We happened to get a video of the bridge jumper, and as I watched it, I noticed that the person got out of their car and ran to jump off the bridge without hesitation or reservation. Their commitment to jump was the equivalent of setting their face.

Imagine if we had some Christians who had faith like that. Better yet, imagine if we had men who were committed like that. Imagine being so committed that we jump full force into the ocean that is God's purpose for each of us.

When a man is committed to his family, children, and friends like that, we see lives changed. That is why I love the story of Boaz in the book of Ruth. Boaz had everything going for him. He had land and property; he had servants and money. But there is something that we may not think about when it comes to Boaz: He was committed to his family and to their ways. It was custom in those times for the family to take care of the widows, even marrying them if need be.

When Boaz found out that Naomi was a relative and thus Ruth was the young woman with her who had been married to Naomi's son, Boaz was committed to see things done properly. He ended up marrying Ruth and taking care of Naomi in the process.

In my case, it was hard for me to commit to a relationship let alone get married and taking care of my wife's mother. Boaz showed great commitment in his keeping God's laws, and because of this, Boaz was included in the lineage of Jesus. This is what it looks like when men commit. They change the lives of those around them while at the same time obeying God.

> Then Boaz said to the elders and all the people, "You are witnesses this day that I have bought from the hand of Naomi all that belonged to Elimelech and all that belonged to Chilion and to Mahlon. Also Ruth the Moabite, the widow of Mahlon, I have bought to be my wife, to perpetuate the name of the dead in his inheritance, that the name of the dead may not be cut off from among his brothers and from the gate of his native place. You are witnesses this day." Then all the people

> who were at the gate and the elders said, "We are witnesses. May the Lord make the woman, who is coming into your house, like Rachel and Leah, who together built up the house of Israel. May you act worthily in Ephrathah and be renowned in Bethlehem, and may your house be like the house of Perez, whom Tamar bore to Judah, because of the offspring that the Lord will give you by this young woman" (Ruth 4:9-12).

The last verse foreshadows Jesus' family tree of which Boaz was a part. But just by reading this, we can see the commitment Boaz made. He did not have to because there was a relative who was closer than he was, but that relative did not have the commitment Boaz had. This is what it looks like when men commit. Communities and lives are changed, and God is glorified.

As I submitted to Jesus, He showed me how committed to me He was. This opened my eyes to my lack of commitment. You might ask how was this a blessing. It was a blessing because once I comprehended His love for me, I was able to see how my lack of commitment had hurt others. Let's just say I was convicted and challenged at the same time. Jesus convicted me by showing me the hurt I had caused. He challenged me to allow Him to do the work in me so I could be a better representative of Him. I wanted to show the Lord once and for all that I did love Him and that meant commitment.

As Jesus changed my heart, I was shown how to commit to my daughter, how to commit to my job, and how to commit to myself. I say to myself because I was not being true to who I really was by my lack of integrity. It is sad to say but now all I can say is thank You, Jesus.

We learn from the twelve disciples that when men commit to something, the world can be changed. When we commit to God and He in turn uses us, we change our homes, our communities, our world. When we examine this concept, we realize why it is so important to God, and why it is referred to so many times in the Bible.

What does your life look like? Is it like mine was—a road littered with hurt and damaged relationships? Or is it one of obedience and love? If you're like I was back then, the good news is it's not too late to change. All you must do is first make the commitment to Jesus. When I say make the commitment to Jesus, I mean a commitment to allow Him to change your heart and renew your mind. This is the start of true commitment and the foundation for a meaningful relationship with Jesus. This is how we learn to love Jesus with all our hearts, strength, mind, and soul as the Bible commands us to do. This is how we learn to commit to things and the people in our lives.

When I finally surrendered to Jesus, I had to show my willingness to commit to Him. When I did that, He changed my life—radically changed my life. My job changed, I started to get promotions, and my income went up. I became committed to my daughter, Ashley, and our relationship did a one hundred eighty degree turnaround.

Then I found the woman that I could commit to—or should I say God found her for me—and she became my wife. It was not until I committed to Jesus that He gave me a ministry, His call on my life to a greater purpose was revealed. This is what it looks like when men commit.

I always say, "If Jesus did it for me, He will do it for you!" Maybe today is a good day to start your journey to authentic manhood. Maybe today is the day that you let Jesus into your life. Maybe you're like I was and you're looking around your life and if you're honest, you admit that what you're doing is not working. You have tried to do it on your own and that didn't work out well. Maybe today is the day to give Jesus a chance, and you too can see what it looks like when a man commits.

> *If you don't plan to live the Christian life totally committed to knowing your God and*

to walking in obedience to Him, then don't begin; for this is what Christianity is all about. It is a change of citizenship, a change of governments, a change of allegiance. If you have no intention of letting Christ rule your life, then forget Christianity; it's not for you. – Kay Arthur

The quote by Kay Arthur is harsh but true. We must look at it with clear hearts and open eyes to grasp the scope of its meaning. Listen, my brother, we cannot afford to get this wrong. Your eternal destiny rests on you getting this right. God foreknew you and those He foreknew He predestined and those He predestined He called, and those He called He justified, and those He justified He glorified (see Romans 8:29-30). That is an amazing summary and shows that God was committed to you from the beginning. It is time for you to commit to a God who gave up everything so you could have relationship with Him. Now that is worth committing to.

LET'S PRAY:

Lord Jesus, I come to You wanting to be the man You created me to be. I know I must surrender my life to You. Right now, Lord, I surrender my life to You. Change and make me into a committed man, Lord. Do in me what is necessary for me to show You that I love You. Take away my fear of being hurt. Help me learn to be committed to You, and then let that permeate my entire life. Allow me to be an agent of change in my small circle of influence. Lord, be glorified in me, in Jesus' name I pray, amen!

SUMMARY POINTS

1. Commitment moves a man from intention to action.
2. When men commit, families and communities are changed.
3. God honors obedience that others refuse.
4. Commitment aligns our lives with God's redemptive purposes.

BIBLE VERSES USED IN THIS CHAPTER:

1 Kings 8:61
Ruth 4:9-12

REFLECTION QUESTIONS

1. Have you left a wake of hurt wherever you have been because of your lack of commitment?
2. What can you do right now to make things right?
3. Do you truly plan to follow Jesus and if so, what does that look like?
4. What do you think are some benefits to your being more committed?

ADDITIONAL STUDY

If we are going to keep it real, commitment cannot remain theoretical. It always shows up in action. We can talk about loving God, honoring our families, and serving others—but commitment is revealed by what we actually do when obedience becomes inconvenient. Jesus never measured commitment by intention; He measured it by follow through.

This chapter confronted an uncomfortable truth: when men commit, lives are changed—but when men refuse to commit, people are left hurt, exposed, and unprotected. Commitment is never private. It always affects someone else. The question is whether our obedience is strong enough to carry responsibility, or whether we step back when the cost becomes personal.

1.
BOAZ
RUTH 2-4

Boaz did not hide behind technicalities or wait for someone else to act. He stepped into responsibility when another man refused to do so. Commitment required Boaz to protect, provide, and follow God's law even when it demanded sacrifice. This is what commitment looks like when a man understands that obedience leaves a legacy.

2.
NEHEMIAH
NEHEMIAH 1-6

Nehemiah faced opposition, exhaustion, and ridicule, yet he refused to abandon the work God had given him. Commitment does not mean the work gets easier–it means you stop giving yourself permission to quit.

3.
MATTHEW 25:21

God does not reward visibility, popularity, or applause. He rewards faithfulness. Commitment may never make you famous, but it will always make you fruitful.

CHAPTER 3

GOD'S COMMITMENT TO US

If I am perturbed by the reproach and misunderstanding that may follow action taken for the good of souls for whom I must give account; if I cannot commit the matter and go on in peace and in silence, remembering Gethsemane and the cross, then I know nothing of Calvary love.

– Amy Carmichael

When he was reviled, he did not revile in return; when he suffered, he did not threaten, but continued entrusting himself to him who judges justly. He himself bore our sins in his body on the tree, that we might die to sin and live to righteousness. By his wounds you have been healed.

– 1 Peter 2:23-25

Do you realize you have put your trust in Jesus and that the God of the universe is now totally committed to you? He loves you, He has sealed His relationship with you by the blood of His own son, Jesus. His blood has covered your sin so now you don't have to worry about a thing in this world.

I was speaking with our men's group recently and a revelation came to me. God calls us as we are to be, not as we are. For example, the angel called Gideon a mighty warrior when He addressed him. However, Gideon did not think of himself like that, but rather thought of himself as being from the least significant tribe and from the least of his clan in the tribe. Yet the angel called him mighty (see Judges 6). Gideon wasn't a mighty warrior yet, but it was who he was going to be. That proves God sees us as we are to be, not where we are.

The Bible says that God predestined you to be adopted sons of God (see Ephesians 1:5). This means that before you were born, God knew you. He knew what you would be and what you would do. When you were in your mess and did not know God, He called you a son. When you were deep in sin, God called you son because He saw you as you are to be.

I am amazed every day when I wake up and think that God called me son when I was far from being or acting like a son. He called me son when I wasn't even thinking about Him. In my most debased situation, God called me son. That blows my mind every day.

That is why when He spoke to me in my bathroom, He asked why I doubted myself when He never had. When I was at the clubs getting drunk, God never doubted me. if this does not speak of love nothing does. If this does not speak of God's commitment to us, nothing does.

I have not even mentioned the obvious commitment that God has made for us: "For God so loved the world, that he gave his only Son, that whoever believes in him should not perish but have eternal life" (John 3:16). Jesus came to die for our sins so that mankind would be redeemed to God our Father. The God of love gave us His Son so that we may be able to have a relationship with Him.

I do not know of anyone who would give their child so that someone else could benefit. That is a commitment of the highest degree. That is next-level commitment. As the verse that I included at the beginning of this chapter says, "by His [Jesus'] stripes we are healed." The commitment that God has made to us is so great because He gave everything for us—He held nothing back that we need to have a relationship with Him.

Not only did God give His Son for us, He also created the earth and gave dominion to man over it. The word *dominion* means to have sovereignty or control. That means God made the earth but then gave control of it to man. God has connected the earth to man in such a way that the earth suffers when man is disobedient. This is the commitment that God has for us. He gave us the world to work and to enjoy, for better or worse. Since God is that committed to us, He wants us to be committed to Him. But this is hard to do. Truth is, we men struggle with commitment. We struggle with it when in relationship with our friends and family, and we struggle with it when we are in relationship with God.

We can look through the Bible and see evidence of God's commitment to man. So, for God the word commitment means love which is described and defined in 1 Corinthians 13:1-13:

> If I speak in the tongues of men and of angels, but have not love, I am a noisy gong or a clanging cymbal. And if I have prophetic powers, and understand all mysteries and all knowledge, and if I have all faith, so as to remove mountains, but have not love, I am nothing. If I give away all I have, and if I deliver up my body to be burned, but have not love, I gain nothing.
>
> Love is patient and kind; love does not envy or boast; it is not arrogant or rude. It does not insist on its own way; it is not irritable or resentful; it does not rejoice at wrongdoing but rejoices with the truth. Love bears all things, believes all things, hopes all things, endures all things.
>
> Love never ends. As for prophecies,

> they will pass away; as for tongues, they will cease; as for knowledge, it will pass away. For we know in part, and we prophesy in part, but when the perfect comes, the partial will pass away. When I was a child, I spoke like a child, I thought like a child, I reasoned like a child. When I became a man, I gave up childish ways. For now we see in a mirror dimly, but then face to face. Now I know in part; then I shall know fully, even as I have been fully known.
>
> So now faith, hope, and love abide, these three; but the greatest of these is love.

In other words, love and commitment go hand and hand. As we look at God's commitment, we see God's love as a perfect example. When we love something, we are more likely to commit to the thing we love. Even if it is a habit or addiction, we cling and commit to the things we love. But also, when we truly love someone, we are then able to commit to that person.

God truly loves us and because He loves us so deeply. I have found that when I talk about God, it isn't long before I talk about love. He has truly committed to us out of love. We will take an entire chapter later to speak about love. But let it suffice for now to conclude that love and commitment go hand and hand.

I was once watching a sermon on the TBN station, and the sermon was about the commitment that Jesus has for us. I prayed before I went to sleep and asked Jesus to visit me in my dreams. That night I found myself standing before Jesus. I could not see His face, but I knew it was Him. He did not speak, and I did not speak to Him. All He did was hug me. The feeling of love that went throughout my entire body was unbelievable. I could not believe that Jesus showed up to give me a hug. I am not anyone special at all, so for Him to show up to give me a hug speaks of His commitment not only to me but also to us.

I spoke about the Father's love, but Jesus had to love as well. He was the one who came down to earth to live the life of a man, to be beaten and ridiculed and then hung on the cross. I often wonder about the kind of commitment it took for Him to go to the cross, knowing that at any time He could have called down a legion of angels to come and defend Him.

We see this clearly in the Garden of Gethsemane. Matthew 26:38-39 reports,

> Then he said to them, "My soul is very sorrowful, even to death; remain here, and watch with me." And going a little farther he fell on his face and prayed, saying, "My Father, if it be possible, let this cup pass from me; nevertheless, not as I will, but as you will."

Here we see the struggle and the commitment in Jesus. He knew what He is about to go through, yet He gave His will over to His Father. Even knowing that He would suffer much Jesus was still committed to His purpose. He had to go to the cross and die so that we could be set free.

Considering this humbles me because Jesus went through all of that for us. My commitment cannot come close to what Jesus shows us about commitment. When measured against the commitment of Jesus, I feel unworthy. Truth is, we should feel unworthy because we are.

This entire book could have been on this one chapter, showing how committed God is to us. If we could follow His example of commitment, we would see a change in the world. We would see our marriages restored. We would see our relationships with our children grow. We would see improvement on our jobs.

God is committed to us!

LET'S PRAY:

Lord, we thank You that You have been and still are committed to us. We pray that we would follow Your example and become more committed to You, to our families, and to our communities. Lord, we ask humbly for You to show us how to be committed men. Show us what it looks like and what the results of being committed men will be. Let the world see the sons of God who are committed to you. We love You, Lord, and we confess that we need You in our lives every second of the day. Have Your way in our lives, Lord, in Jesus' name, amen!

SUMMARY POINTS

1. God committed to me before I ever committed to Him.
2. God sees me as who I am becoming, not just who I am.
3. The cross is the ultimate expression of divine commitment.
4. God's love proves commitment is unconditional.

BIBLE VERSES USED IN THIS CHAPTER:

1 Peter 2:23-25
Judges 6
John 3:16
1 Corinthians 13:1-13
Matthew 26:38-39

REFLECTION QUESTIONS

1. When you look at your life, how has God shown His commitment to you?
2. How does the commitment of God influence and impact you?
3. Does seeing God's commitment to your life challenge you to be more committed?
4. How does reading about God's commitment make you feel?

ADDITIONAL STUDY

Before we ask why commitment is so difficult for us, we must be honest about this: God has never failed to commit to us. Even when we were inconsistent, distracted, or rebellious, God remained faithful. If we struggle with commitment, it is not because God has modeled inconsistency—it is because we underestimate the depth of His love.

This chapter directed us to stop projecting our failures onto God. He does not abandon us. He does not waver. He does not walk away. When we see God's commitment clearly, our excuses lose their power. Love this deep demands a response.

1.
GIDEON
JUDGES 6-7

God called Gideon a mighty warrior while Gideon was still hiding. God commits to who we are becoming, not who we currently believe ourselves to be. That truth should both comfort and challenge us.

2.
ROMANS 5:6-8

Christ died for us while we were still sinners. That is commitment without conditions, without guarantees, and without negotiation. Love like that removes every excuse for half-hearted devotion.

3.
ISAIAH 49:15-16

God's commitment to us is permanent. We are engraved on His hands. We are not forgotten, overlooked, or misplaced. When we doubt God's faithfulness, we are not seeing Him clearly.

CHAPTER 4

THE CALL TO COMMIT

To fall in love with God is the greatest romance; to seek him the greatest adventure; to find him, the greatest human achievement.
– Saint Augustine

I appeal to you therefore, brothers, by the mercies of God, to present your bodies as a living sacrifice, holy and acceptable to God, which is your spiritual worship. Do not be conformed to this world, but be transformed by the renewal of your mind, that by testing you may discern what is the will of God, what is good and acceptable and perfect.
– Romans 12:1-2

The call to commit comes to every man. This passage says that we are to present our bodies as a living sacrifice, going on to say that this is our spiritual worship. So, if I am reading this correctly, God wants us to be a living sacrifice to Him. The word *sacrifice* means a person surrendering a possession as an offering to God. Talk about commitment. This means that we are not called to be what the world has made us to be.

We are made to be a sacrifice to God, holy unto Him for his use and purpose. This will take a commitment like we have never made before.

The Hebrew word for *commitment* has a connotation of trust. The Greek word for commitment has two applications for it. It means to place alongside or to deposit someplace or someone as a trust or for protection. This gives us a different understanding of the word. God has called us to be entrusted in Him and in this passage, He says we are not be conformed to the world, but to be transformed by the renewing of our minds so that we may be able to test what is His good and perfect for our lives. If we commit to God and His will, then we will know what it is, which is in part the reason why we don't commit in the first place. We are afraid of what that will may be. *Will I be poor? Will I lose my job? Will I have to go on the missions field?*

So many of us become like the prodigal son who took his portion of the inheritance and went off to a far country where he squandered all he had until he was in need. Then a famine came into the land, and no one gave him anything so he hired himself out feeding the pigs. He was so destitute that he longed for the pods that the pigs were eating. Then something supernatural happened.

The scripture in Luke 15 says that the prodigal son came to himself. He thought to himself that the servants in his Father's house had more food than he did. So he arose and go back and said to his father, "I have sinned against God and you. Make me as one of your servants." My rendition is a paraphrase, but if you want to read it, you can go to Luke 15 and read it for yourself.

I have heard many say that the prodigal son went home because he was hungry. One day as I was studying this passage, the Holy Spirit said to me, "Yes, the prodigal son was hungry but it was the hunger that made him come to himself. If he had not been hungry, he would not have come to himself."

What is interesting about this parable is that in order for the prodigal son to come to himself means that before that, he was not himself. His wild living turned him in to someone else, but *that wasn't who he was.* I do not mean to say that he had some kind of split personality. I am saying that the wild and crazy living changed him and he was not who he was when he left his father's house. Therefore, he had to come to himself again before he could go home.

And this is what the passage is saying to us. We are to present ourselves as a holy sacrifice. I suggest that the world and our wild living has changed us just like it did the son in the parable. We are not functioning in a manner consistent with the image of God in which we were created. Now in order for us to take on the image of our Father, we have to come to ourselves and the way that God brings us to ourselves is by allowing us to go through a season of famine. If we squander our finances God puts us in a famine. If we squander our relationships, God puts us a famine in that area.

The Lord knows if we get hungry enough, we will come to our senses and come home. Then and only then will we be the committed sons that our Father has called us to be. I bet that the prodigal son was a very committed son after his return.

I purposely did not finish the parable, skipping over the best part. Picking up where I left off, the passage says that while he was a long way off, the Father saw him. This excites me when I think about it. I can imagine the Father, day after day, week after week, looking down the road for His son to come home. The Father had to be looking in order for Him to see the son from a long way off.

On that day he saw him, the father must have said to himself, *I know that walk. I know the way he's carrying his head and swings his arms. That is my son who was dead and is alive.* The Father runs and hugs His son and as the son is saying his rehearsed speech, the Father tells the servant to go get a robe and put it on him. He also directed him to put a ring on his finger and shoes on his feet. Finally, he ordered that the fatted calf be killed so they can celebrate, for the son who was dead but is now alive.

This is what the Heavenly Father does each and every time one of His prodigal sons makes their way home. The prodigal son was called to commit but he had to be hungry first. My question to you is: Are you hungry? Are you tired of trying to live in a far-off country? Have you squandered all you have on wild living and now find yourself in a famine? There is a call for you to commit to the Father, to come home and restore God's image in you that was taken away from God's creation. There is a call to be the son of God but this will require nothing less than complete commitment.

I have shared a lot about myself and my spiritual journey in my previous books. I was a prodigal son lost in a far-off country. I was living a wild and crazy life. In previous chapters, I spoke of the hurt I caused. But I was not myself and I had no idea who I was until Jesus called me by name. I was bankrupt in spirit and mind. I had to come to myself and remember that I needed to be in the Father's house.

There came a time when I was forty years old and my mother passed away. At that time, I made a commitment to serve Jesus for the rest of my life.

I made that commitment in part to honor my mother because she was a woman of God.

But for the most part, I always knew that God would call me back to Him. However, I had to come to a place where I came to myself. I realized that I had never been committed to Jesus, but it was time to do so—to go all in. If I can suggest, my brother, that if you have not committed to Jesus, it's time to come to yourself. It's time to come home. The word committed means to give of yourself wholeheartedly.

Let me finish this chapter with this thought. I was reading Luke chapter 22 where Peter denied Jesus three times. What caught my attention was when the third denial occurred, Scripture says that the rooster crowed, and Jesus looked at Peter. It was then that Peter remembered and wept bitterly.

What caught my attention was that Peter was under the spell of fear. When the gaze of grace caught the eyes of Peter, he came to himself. The passage says that Peter remembered and wept bitterly. I was blown away that with one look from Jesus, Peter came to himself. We know that Peter goes on to be a powerful leader in the church, that Peter would be committed from that point on for the rest of his life. This is the type of commitment I want. How about you?

LET'S PRAY:

Lord, I invite You into my heart. Lord, You know of my lukewarm condition. But, Lord, I want to be committed to You. I want nothing short of all of You. Holy Spirit, I am inviting You into my heart. Please teach me to love you the way I should. Teach me to be the man I am called to be–a committed son of God. My desire is to glorify You in my life. Lord, I commit to You in this moment. Have Your way in me. These things I pray in the mighty name of Jesus, amen!

SUMMARY POINTS

1. Commitment requires surrender, not control.
2. God often uses famine to awaken sons to their identity.
3. Coming to God begins with coming to ourselves.
4. Restoration follows repentance and commitment.

BIBLE VERSES USED IN THIS CHAPTER:

Romans 12:1-2
Luke 15:11-32

REFLECTION QUESTIONS

1. How can you come to yourself?
2. Have you ever truly thought about what commitment level you have?
3. Are you being called to a deeper commitment in Jesus? If so, how and what will you do?
4. How does being committed to Jesus effect the rest of your life?

ADDITIONAL STUDY

God's call to commitment often comes after we have exhausted our own way of living. Hunger, loss, and failure are not signs that God has abandoned us—they are often signs that He is calling us home. Commitment begins when we stop pretending that life without God is working.

This chapter confronted the moment when excuses run out. God does not force commitment, but He will allow circumstances to expose our need for Him. Coming to ourselves is often painful, but it is always merciful.

1.
THE PRODIGAL SON
LUKE 15:11-32

The son did not return home until he became hungry enough to face the truth. Hunger has a way of stripping away illusions. Commitment begins when we admit that life apart from the Father is not freedom.

2.
PETER'S RESTORATION
LUKE 22; JOHN 21

Peter's failure didn't disqualify him—his refusal to stay broken restored him. One look from Jesus brought Peter back to himself. Commitment often begins with repentance, not perfection.

3.
HEBREWS 12:11

God disciplines His sons because He loves them. Discipline is not punishment—it's formation. Commitment grows when we submit to God's correction instead of resisting it.

CHAPTER 5

THE CHOICE TO FOLLOW JESUS

When we come to Christ, we're no longer the most important person in the world to us; Christ is. Instead of living only for ourselves, we have a higher goal: to live for Jesus.
– Billy Graham

Then Jesus told his disciples, "If anyone would come after me, let him deny himself and take up his cross and follow me."
– Matthew 16:24

This passage says it all about commitment. "If anyone comes after me, let him deny himself and take up his cross and follow me." In order to take up your cross and follow Jesus, you will have to be committed. This is not a call to a part-time relationship with Jesus. This will also take a choice to follow Him totally and in every area of life.

In order for us to better understand this, let's look at someone in the Bible who carried his cross for Jesus. The Apostle Paul started off badly but ended very well. As a Jew, he hated the followers of Jesus. In fact, we are told in Acts 9 that he was on his way to Damascus to arrest some when he had his encounter with Jesus. This encounter left him blind and others had to lead him by the hand to his destination. Three days later, he encountered a man by the name of Ananias. It's best to let Scripture tell you the rest of the story:

> Now there was a disciple at Damascus named Ananias. The Lord said to him in a vision, "Ananias." And he said, "Here I am, Lord." And the Lord said to him, "Rise and go to the street called Straight, and at the house of Judas look for a man of Tarsus named Saul, for behold, he is praying, and he has seen in a vision a man named Ananias come in and lay his hands on him so that he might regain his sight." But Ananias answered, "Lord, I have heard from many about this man, how much evil he has done to your saints at Jerusalem. And here he has authority from the chief priests to bind all who call on your name." But the Lord said to him, "Go, for he is a chosen instrument of mine to carry my name before the Gentiles and kings and the

> children of Israel. For I will show him how much he must suffer for the sake of my name." So Ananias departed and entered the house. And laying his hands on him he said, "Brother Saul, the Lord Jesus who appeared to you on the road by which you came has sent me so that you may regain your sight and be filled with the Holy Spirit." And immediately something like scales fell from his eyes, and he regained his sight. Then he rose and was baptized; and taking food, he was strengthened (Acts 9:10-19).

You may be thinking that Saul/Paul was not committed, that he was abducted or overpowered with no choice in the matter. It may look that way as you read the passage, but Saul/Paul was committed to God even though his zeal wasn't taking him in the right direction. Jesus redirected Saul/Paul toward the truth of the gospel so that his zeal and commitment for Judaism and God would not be wasted or misplaced.

To me it was a stroke of genius by Jesus. He took the enemy's sharpest tool away from him and used him for His own good. By the way, even though Saul/Paul had this encounter with Jesus, he still had his free will. In other words, Saul/Paul could have stood his ground and refused. After all, there were companions with

Saul/Paul that day who saw the light, but as far as we know, were not impacted by it.

But who can refuse Jesus when they have had a true encounter with Him. I'm convinced that if you have had a true encounter with Jesus, change is mandatory and inevitable. It's impossible to have an encounter with Jesus and remain the same. It's in His nature to change people. So, if you have had an encounter with Jesus and remained the same, you have not had a legitimate encounter with Jesus. You may have had an idea of Jesus but not a true encounter. Paul had a true encounter with Jesus, and it changed his direction and perspective.

All the apostles had a heavy cross to carry but in my opinion, Paul had the heaviest of all. Peter had a heavy cross to carry as well, but we do not see Peter planting churches all over the world. We do not see anyone else being sent to speak to kings. Paul's cross was heavy indeed, but one that he was committed to carry. I love what Paul says as he is coming to the end of his life.

> For I am already being poured out as a drink offering, and the time of my departure has come. I have fought the good fight, I have finished the race, I have kept the faith. Henceforth there is laid up for me the crown of righteousness, which the Lord, the righteous judge, will award to me on

> that day, and not only to me but also to all who have loved his appearing (2 Timothy 4:6-8).

Now that is a man who carried his cross for Jesus. That is a man who was a committed servant of Christ. We should all hope that at the end of our lives we can say, "I have been poured out as a drink offering." How powerful these words are that Paul stated. These are words of a man who had carried his cross and was totally committed to Jesus. This was the choice of Paul to follow his Lord and Savior.

We are all called to follow Jesus, but it's a choice to do so. I assume because you picked up this book that you have made the choice to follow Jesus. But we make choices all the time that we are not committed to. Sometimes things seem like a good idea, so we make the decision to commit to things we do not really care about.

So, we have come this far, and it must be a question in your mind of how to commit to Jesus. How did Paul commit to Jesus? How did Peter, John, Matthew, Phillip, and the rest of the disciples commit to Jesus? They committed because they loved Jesus. If you think about it, you have committed to things life because you love them. The choice to follow Jesus has to be a choice to have a relationship with Him because you love Him. This is a book directed toward men, and what I am really talking about is love.

I have found this is the main reason so many men do not commit–they are afraid of love. That was true in my life for a long time. I was afraid to love because love had hurt me, so I decided that I would not give my heart to anyone. I would protect my heart at all cost, and because of that attitude, I in turn hurt many people. That meant I was also unable to give my heart to Jesus.

Women get this because the books they read are about love. They talk about love all the time with each other. They have a natural tendency toward being able to love freely, whereas men do not. In fact, we have been taught to run from love. This is why I have written this book because, brothers, we're losing. We're losing our families and children for lack of love.

The reality of it is that the love of the world is a wimpy, lackluster love. The love that Jesus shows and gives is a manly love that can endure. In case you did not know, our God is a warrior. He fights for what He loves. He protects what He loves. He provides for what He loves. He defends what He loves.

Our God is not offended or afraid to show His love. Truth be told, it's manly to show love to others. Let me say it again: it's manly to show love. And it will take love to answer the call to follow Jesus. It will take your love in order to carry your cross as part of your commitment to Jesus.

This is why I love David of the Old Testament so much. David loved God more than anything or anyone else. He wrote poems and hymns to God. David did not do anything without seeking God. In fact, the time David did not seek God, he made a mistake and slept with another man's wife. Then he doubled down on it and has her husband killed. This is why I love the Bible because it gives us the truth.

But even though David did those things, he was still known as a man after God's own heart—a man who chose to follow God and a man who God blessed so much that our Savior came from his lineage. If that does not signify the kind of commitment David had, nothing does.

The question to you, my brother, is what decisions have you made to follow Jesus? And will you follow through with them because you love Him?

LET'S PRAY:

Lord, let me be a man of God. Lord, I want to be a man that is committed to You. God, I know that if I am committed to You, then I will be committed to my family. Lord, I know that I will also be committed to my job and community. I choose to commit to You and surrender all that I am to You. I ask that You come into my life in the mighty name of Jesus.

SUMMARY POINTS

1. Following Jesus is a daily choice.
2. Commitment requires denying self and embracing obedience.
3. Love for Jesus empowers endurance.
4. A true encounter with Christ leads to change.

BIBLE VERSES USED IN THIS CHAPTER:

Matthew 16:24
Acts 9:10-19
2 Timothy 4:6-8

REFLECTION QUESTIONS

1. If I look at my walk with Jesus, does it look like I am committed?
2. How can I seek Jesus more in my everyday life?
3. What does God expect from me in the area of commitment?
4. Have I made an honest choice to follow Jesus?

ADDITIONAL STUDY

Following Jesus is not an emotional decision—it is a lifelong choice. Many men admire Jesus, respect Jesus, and even talk about Jesus, but fewer are willing to deny themselves and follow Him wherever He leads. Jesus never hid the cost of discipleship because He knew that anything less than full commitment would eventually collapse under pressure.

This chapter asked a difficult question: have we truly chosen to follow Jesus, or have we chosen a version of Christianity that allows us to remain in control? Love for Jesus is proven not by words, but by obedience. When following Him costs us comfort, reputation, or control, that is when the authenticity of our commitment is revealed.

1.
PAUL'S CONVERSION
ACTS 9

Paul's encounter with Jesus didn't just change his beliefs—it changed his direction. He surrendered his plans, his status, and his future. A real encounter with Jesus always demands change. Anything less is not discipleship.

2.
THE RICH YOUNG RULER
MARK 10:17-22

This man wanted eternal life, but he would not release control. Jesus exposed the one thing that mattered most to him. Commitment often breaks down at the point where surrender becomes personal.

3.
GALATIANS 2:20

A committed man no longer lives for himself. His life is no longer his own. Following Jesus means dying to self so that Christ can truly live through us.

CHAPTER 6

THE DIFFERENCE BETWEEN KNOWING AND FOLLOWING

When Jesus had spoken these words, he lifted up his eyes to heaven, and said, "Father, the hour has come; glorify your Son that the Son may glorify you, since you have given him authority over all flesh, to give eternal life to all whom you have given him. And this is eternal life, that they know you, the only true God, and Jesus Christ whom you have sent.

– John 17:1-3

"[It is] our inclination to replace Jesus' call to deny ourselves, take up our crosses and follow him. We replace his call with a self-serving path in which we deny our neighbors, take up our comforts and follow our dreams."

– Scott Sauls

This is a chapter that I am excited to write because it has been on my heart for a while. The theme is knowing the difference between being a follower of Jesus and knowing Jesus. The challenge I have is where to start, so I will start with the first and end with the second. Let's talk about what it means to follow Jesus.

When I think of following someone, I think of a band or sports team that I enjoy. I follow and watch them. I like the songs or the team. The problem with following something is that I never make a true connection with the thing I am following. Here is an example of what I am saying.

I like Elevation Worship, and I listen to their songs; they are an anointed worship team. But it does not matter how many of their songs I download or how many concerts I go to; I will never know them. Because I follow them from a distance, I can walk away from them at any time.

I feel as though there are too many Christians who are followers of Jesus like that. Our walk is like going to a football game or favorite sports event. We sit in the stands, and we cheer and shout. We even paint our faces and wear their swag in support. But when the event or game is over, I get in my car and go home, never meeting or knowing anyone who played in the game—or who was a fellow spectator for that matter. I follow them from a distance and whenever I want, I can walk away.

Jesus tells us to follow Him, but that kind of following should lead to knowing. The passage I mention above says that they know You and Jesus Christ. It does not say to follow God and Jesus it says to know.

> "Not everyone who says to me, 'Lord, Lord,' will enter the kingdom of heaven, but the one who does the will of my Father who is in heaven. On that day many will say to me, 'Lord, Lord, did we not prophesy in your name, and cast out demons in your name, and do many mighty works in your name?' And then will I declare to them, 'I never knew you; depart from me, you workers of lawlessness'" (Matthew 7:21-23).

This in my opinion is the most frightening verse in the Bible. Jesus is clearly speaking to some people who have worked in the Kingdom. They have cast out demons in the name of Jesus, but they lack one thing. They do not know Jesus, and this gets them evicted from the presence of Jesus who says, "I never knew you." Is it possible that these people were followers of Jesus who never took the time to get to know Jesus? They never let Jesus know them and never truly had a relationship with Him. This frightens me because Jesus said that many people would say these things and He would still tell them He never knew them.

This tells us that Jesus wants us to do more than follow Him. He wants to know us and He wants us to know Him. This is called relationship and is at the core of this book. In order to form a relationship to Jesus, you must be committed. You must obey His commands and not just follow Him; you must know Him. And we cannot know Him unless we are in a committed relationship with Him.

Let me illustrate this for you. Imagine that you are married, but you don't live with your wife, only occasionally seeing her. When you see each other, you have small talk but there is never any real depth to the conversations. You even go as far as to provide for her, paying her mortgage or rent. But truth is, you do not know her in the way a man and a women should know each other when they are married. There is no depth to the relationship, and it only exists in the shallow regions of your mind.

This is what we do with Jesus. We go to church on Sundays and even lead the ushers or armor bearers. We will go to the Bible studies and may even lead one, but never let Jesus get close or never get close to Him. My brother, this is a scary place to be because Jesus has already said that He will tell many that He never knew them. This has become my rally cry for His sons to truly know Him so in the end we hear "Well done good and faithful servant."

I pastor a church named Rally Point Church and even though we are a young church, this is our rally cry. Our pillars are prayer and discipleship. Prayer because through it you build a relationship with Jesus, and through discipleship we learn to be obedient to Jesus. It has not always been easy but it has been rewarding as we have gotten closer to Jesus. We have seen Him do great work in and through us as we have gotten closer to Him. I will tell you the same thing I tell my congregation almost every week. We have to get this right; we cannot afford to get this wrong. Our eternal destiny is resting on our getting this right. It's not easy to get to know Jesus. It will require a heart that is surrendered and a spirit that is committed.

If I can be honest with you, I was once a follower of Jesus. I got saved but I was still living the same life as I was before I met the Lord. I did not know that total surrender is what I had to do, was what He was after. Plus, I had been told again and again that Jesus would do the work, so in my mind all I had to do was sit back and watch God.

It's true that Jesus does all the work but there is a part that you must play. That part is to be available and to be willing to allow Jesus into your heart. Before I knew that, I was walking around with a hard heart. I would not let anyone into my life especially into my heart. Am I reading your mail when I write this? I was a typical male who had served in the army and been a state trooper. I was wise in the ways of the world but not wise in the ways of the Lord. It was not until I allowed Jesus to touch my heart concerning my daughter Ashley that I began to know the truth and be confronted with my hardness.

The Lord showed me why my relationship with my daughter was so rocky, and the problem was me. The Lord showed me how I didn't hear her heart when she was younger. I was not a great dad to my little girl at the time. Brother, that hurt me to the core and it broke me down. That's when my hard heart started to melt.

Eventually Jesus restored my relationship with my daughter because I was willing to let Jesus do a work in me to change me. I had to commit to being a father to my daughter. I thought I had been one but after Jesus shed light on what I was, I saw that I was severely lacking.

This is how we can handle our relationship with Jesus. It is a casual non-committal relationship that has no power or substance. But just like my daughter Ashley wanted a relationship with her father, our Savior wants a relationship with us. He wants to know us and for us to know Him. I pray that you open your heart in surrender to Jesus at this very moment. I pray that the Spirit of God will shine some light on your relationship so you can see where you're lacking.

It's a good and important thing to follow Jesus, but that following should lead to knowing Him. If somehow you jumped off the train before you got to know Him, you may be in danger of hearing those ominous words: "I never knew you."

> May the God of hope fill you with all joy and peace in believing, so that by the power of the Holy Spirit you may abound in hope (Romans 15:13).
>
> Then he said to them, "Go your way. Eat the fat and drink sweet wine and send portions to anyone who has nothing ready, for this day is holy to our Lord. And do not be grieved, for the joy of the Lord is your strength" (Nehemiah 8:10).

Joy is the result of knowing Jesus. He gives us joy in the power of the Spirit and that joy becomes our strength. May the God of hope fill you with all joy and peace in believing. This is what it means to know Jesus as your personal Savior: Jesus becomes your Savior because of the relationship you have with Him. Think of it: You get to know the Lord of the universe and He wants to know you. That should have you running around your living room or office right now.

It's crazy to think that the King of kings, and the Lord of lords wants to be intimate with us. He wants to know us and wants us to know Him. If that does not make you feel some kind of way, nothing will. This is what it means to be committed; this is what it means to know Jesus.

LET'S PRAY:

Lord God, I want to know You more than ever before. I want You to know me and I want more of You. Show me the way to intimacy with You. Teach me to pray more effectively and bring me to an understanding of Your word. Lord Jesus, I want more; I want to know You. Here I am, Lord. Direct me in the right ways. I pray these things in the name of Jesus, amen!

SUMMARY POINTS

1. It is possible to follow Jesus publicly without knowing Him personally.
2. Relationship requires obedience, surrender, and intimacy.
3. Religious activity cannot replace commitment.
4. Eternal life is defined by knowing God.

BIBLE VERSES USED IN THIS CHAPTER:

John 17:1-3
Matthew 7:21-23
Romans 15:13
Nehemiah 8:10

REFLECTION QUESTIONS

1. Are you just a follower or do you know Jesus?
2. What can you do to get to know Jesus more?
3. Are you a casual fan of Jesus?
4. Are you afraid to hear "I never knew you"?
5. List five things you can do right now to be a true son of God.

ADDITIONAL STUDY

This chapter should unsettle us. It is possible to follow Jesus publicly, serve faithfully, and still never know Him personally. Jesus' warning in Matthew 7 was not directed at atheists—it was directed at people who thought they were safe. Relationship, not religious activity, is what separates knowing Jesus from merely following Him at a distance.

Keeping it real means admitting that proximity to Jesus does not equal intimacy. Knowledge about Him does not replace obedience to Him. Jesus is not impressed by activity that avoids relationship.

1.
MARY AND MARTHA
LUKE 10:38-42

Martha was busy doing things for Jesus, but Mary chose to be with Him. Activity without intimacy eventually leads to frustration and burnout. Jesus made it clear which choice mattered most.

2.
MATTHEW 7:21-23

These words should stop us cold. Jesus did not deny their activity—He denied their relationship. Works done without intimacy will never substitute for knowing Him.

3.
PHILIPPIANS 3:8-10

Paul willingly laid aside status, reputation, and achievement so that he could know Christ. That kind of knowing requires surrender, not performance.

CHAPTER 7

THE RESULT OF KNOWING JESUS

When Jesus had spoken these words, he lifted up his eyes to heaven, and said, "Father, the hour has come; glorify your Son that the Son may glorify you, since you have given him authority over all flesh, to give eternal life to all whom you have given him. And this is eternal life, that they know you, the only true God, and Jesus Christ whom you have sent. I glorified you on earth, having accomplished the work that you gave me to do. And now, Father, glorify me in your own presence with the glory that I had with you before the world existed."

– John 17:1-5

To be loved but not known is comforting but superficial. To be known and not loved is our greatest fear. But to be fully known and truly loved is, well, a lot like being loved by God. It is what we need more than anything. It liberates us from pretense, humbles us out of our self-righteousness, and fortifies us for any difficulty life can throw at us.

– Timothy Keller

I include this passage from the Bible to start this chapter because it is so powerful. Can you see how committed the Father was to Jesus and Jesus was to the Father? This is the same commitment they want with us. What we are about to talk about is probably my favorite portion of this book because I get to tell you about the awesome results that come from knowing Jesus. This is going to be a powerful chapter, and I hope that you receive as much revelation as I have while writing this.

> But he said to me, "My grace is sufficient for you, for my power is made perfect in weakness." Therefore I will boast all the more gladly of my weaknesses, so that the power of Christ may rest upon me (2 Corinthians 12:8-9).

We do not know what Paul was referring to or what he was praying about. What we do know is that it was a thorn that he wanted removed. I found that when I got saved and started following Jesus, there were some things that He took away right away, and other things that He allowed to stay. Was that your experience? Some of my old problems and temptations disappeared overnight but some remained.

We will have thorns, and we will go through things, but what Jesus said is true: His grace is sufficient for us. In the Bible, grace is defined as God's unmerited favor, goodness, and lovingkindness extended to humanity, especially to those who are undeserving. What a powerful gift this is that God has given us through Jesus Christ.

But today can we look a little more closely at what grace is? Can we talk about grace so that we can walk in the right way before God? It's true that grace is God's unmerited favor, goodness, and lovingkindness given to us, but from what Paul has written, grace is much more.

When I was a young Christian, I equated grace with being given a free pass. It's true that through grace we have all been given a pass. But grace is much more, and I wonder how many are walking around missing what grace has to offer? I will be honest that when someone would say I am saved by grace or covered by grace, it didn't really help me. Don't get me wrong, I understood that it was the grace of God that we have a Savior in Jesus. But what does it really mean to have the unmerited favor of God?

When I think of grace, I think of the song written by John Newton titled *Amazing Grace*. When we look at the first verse, what do we see?

> *Amazing grace, how sweet the sound, that saved a wretch like me! I once was lost, but now am found, was blind, but now I see.*

It was and is still a beautiful song with awesome lyrics. How amazing grace is that saved a wretch like me. Grace found us and saved us. *Unmerited* means we did not deserve it but it was given. Favor means it was an act of kindness that is beyond what is due or usual. But in the song, it says that grace did something. Paul stated that grace is more than unmerited favor. I look at favor differently than the description I gave you. My definition of favor is a closeness that allows you to have everything. So if grace is favor underserved, then the God we serve has done something supernatural for us that most of us do not understand.

The primary Hebrew word for *grace* or *favor* is *chen* (חֵן), often translated as a gift given with delight, charm, or beauty, and a divine influence or power. In a biblical context, *chen* signifies a divine influence or power from God that works to change a person's capacities for work, suffering, or obedience.

Let me talk about the fact that 1) grace is enough; 2) grace is power in weakness; and 3) grace is upon us.

1. Grace is enough.

"*My grace is sufficient for you*"

In the Bible, Peter walked on water until he got scared and began to sink. Jesus saved him and said, "You of little faith, why did you doubt?" Peter didn't need perfect faith to walk on the water; he just needed to trust.

Like Peter, we often doubt and worry,

thinking our faith isn't enough. But like Peter, Jesus invites us to step out, reminding us that His grace is sufficient for us, even when our faith feels shaky.

Jesus Himself said that His grace is sufficient. I am learning that the gospel is enough, and grace is sufficient. The thorn was given to Paul to keep him from being conceited. Imagine the Lord showing you something so great that you know you're special. You might become like Joseph after his father gave him the multicolored coat. He became conceited because his father had shown him that he loved him more than the others.

In the same way, Paul saw something so great that he understood how much God loved and favored him. So, God had to allow a thorn so Paul would not become conceited and prideful. It makes you wonder if that is the reason Jesus doesn't remove some of the problems in us. The purpose of the thorn was to produce humility in Paul, ensuring he would rely on God's strength rather than his own after receiving extraordinary spiritual insights. God allowed a messenger of Satan to harass Paul, Paul prayed that it would be taken away, but God did not do so.

Have you ever had something that you wished God would take away? I know I have, but I have learned that it keeps me humble. It keeps me in a place where I can never claim anything I have is because of what I have done. It reminds me that without Jesus I would be a nothing with nothing. His grace is sufficient and more than enough for me and for you. I am excited about grace, but I have learned that lesson because I have had to rely on the grace in the midst of the burden or thorn that would not go away.

The Hebrew word for *grace* means *influence* or *power*. Think about that for a minute. Jesus told Paul that His grace is sufficient. In other words, "My influence, my power is enough for you." If you aren't excited after reading that, you have not caught this definition of grace. That makes sense to me.

I am sure you have heard the saying that when you enter the room as a Christian, the atmosphere should change. Yes, it changes but not because you're in the room but the grace that you carry is in the room. The power of God has entered the space, and the atmosphere must bend to the will of God. This is a result of knowing Jesus.

2. Grace is power in weakness.

"My power is made perfect in weakness" (2 Corinthians 12:9).

In the early days of the church I pastor, there was a pastor who was struggling to connect with his youth group. No matter what he tried—ice cream socials, game nights, sermons—they just didn't respond. Then one Sunday, he shared a personal story of failure and how God's grace had carried him through. The kids laughed, cried, and finally opened up to him. That pastor learned that grace isn't just a theological concept; it's the glue that holds our relationships together, and in sharing our weaknesses, we exhibit its sufficiency.

Here is where we start to truly understand what grace is. Jesus told Paul that His power is made perfect in weakness. So here is the deal, the Lord allows some things to remain in us so we will continue to rely on Him, because it is in that reliance that God's favor rests on us.

When we realize that we are weak and can only survive because of the presence of a loving God, we will see His power in our lives. That's because His power is made perfect in our weakness. So, if Jesus was saying to Paul that His grace was sufficient, then Jesus was saying to Paul that His grace is the power.

"M grace is the power to get you past the thorn. My grace is the power to get you through the storm. My grace is the power to heal you. My grace is My favor in your life. It is everything that comes with My power." His grace is sufficient. That gives us a whole new understanding of grace. When Jesus says His grace is sufficient, He is not lying.

When we don't know this, we cannot walk in the true power of God.

- If you have the grace of God, you have the power to break addiction.
- If you have the grace of God, you have the power to step out of depression.
- If you have the grace of God, you have the power to heal broken relationships.
- If you have the grace of God, you have the power to break oppression.

Jesus said His grace is sufficient. You don't need anything else when you have grace.

I am walking with power because I have the grace of my Lord and Savior. That is why I do not stress as easily as before because God is working things out through the power of grace. Pause right now and thank God for grace. During your walk with God, you're going to run into situations that may seem to be too much for you to handle. Know that the power of grace will get you through.

The Greek word for power is *dunamis*, which means *power, miracle, ability, miraculous power, strength, explosive.* Are you getting the gist of what grace is? It's power, pure and simple.

Brother, you should be walking around singing that old song by Snap "I've got the power." His grace is sufficient because His power is made perfect in weakness. Grace is the power to walk in the calling of Jesus. This is what knowing Jesus is all about. Can you see now why this is my favorite chapter?

We should desire to know Jesus. He desires for us to know Him in an intimate way because the result is that we receive His grace in power. I have one more point to make on grace.

3. Grace is upon us.

I will boast all the more gladly of my weakness.
So the power of Christ may rest upon me
(2 Corinthians 12:9).

In establishing the early church, Paul faced opposition and persecution. Instead of hiding his struggles, he openly talked about them, saying he would boast in his weaknesses. This not only strengthened his faith but also encouraged others. His transparency became a testimony that God's power shines brightest when we admit we can't do it alone.

I love that Paul said he would boast all the more gladly of his weakness so the power of Christ would rest upon him. You thought your weakness disqualified you, but it is actually what qualifies you. You thought your weakness was what hinders you but it is what allows the power of Jesus to rest upon you. That is the reason you can walk through some things that others can't walk through.

Therefore, stop asking Jesus why He left those things in your life that you can't seem to overcome. He did it because it is what keeps you humble and then His power can rest upon you. He can then work His power through you. That is why I don't stress because I know "I'm just a nobody trying to tell everybody about somebody who changes anybody" as the song says.

And in my weakness God's power is made perfect. I echo Paul that I will boast of my weakness so that Christ's power may rest on me.

If you have grace, give the Lord some praise! Imagine how special you are that Jesus, the Son of God, has chosen to give you grace—the unmerited favor of God. The power of God has been given to you and you did not earn or deserve it. Now because of the blood of Jesus you have been given grace. This grace is upon you and within you.

Stop walking around as if you have no power. Stop looking at your weakness as if it disqualifies from following and serving God. Instead boast all the more because you know that the power of Jesus is made perfect in your weakness.

> Let us then with confidence draw near to the throne of grace, that we may receive mercy and find grace to help in time of need (Hebrews 4:16).

Some versions say, "Let us come to the

throne of grace with boldness." Think about that for a second. The writer of Hebrews says there is a throne of grace. In every kingdom, the throne that the king sits on is the seat of power in that kingdom. May we come boldly before the seat of power, the seat of God's Kingdom—before the throne of grace. Here is what Peter had to say about grace.

> And after you have suffered a little while, the God of all grace, who has called you to his eternal glory in Christ, will himself restore, confirm, strengthen, and establish you (1 Peter 5:10).

It is the power of grace that strengthens and transforms you. Jesus has given you His authority and in that authority resides His grace. When you grasp this, you will start looking at your weakness differently. I am not a good speaker, at least not in my opinion. But when I start to share the word of God His grace, His power comes upon me.

> "The Spirit of the Lord is upon me, because he has anointed me to proclaim good news to the poor. He has sent me to proclaim liberty to the captives and recovering of sight to the blind, to set at liberty those who are oppressed" (Luke 4:18).

If we were in the same room right now, we

would be high fiving each other. Let me end this chapter with one final thought:

> For the sake of Christ, then, I am content with weaknesses, insults, hardships, persecutions, and calamities. For when I am weak, then I am strong (2 Corinthians 12:10).

There will be times when everything seems to come against you. When it does, know that when you're at your weakest, the power of Jesus is made perfect. In the areas of your life that you look at and think you are not good enough or don't have the ability, that is when grace kicks in and the power of God makes up the difference.

It is like you had a meter measuring your ability and you could only fill the meter up about a quarter of the way. The grace of Jesus then comes in and fills it the rest of the way. Therefore, be content in your weakness, knowing that His power is made perfect in that place.

If you are reading this and you have been battling with difficult situations in your life, or if you have been looking at your weakness as if it is what stops you or holds you back, I want to pray for you. Maybe you haven't stepped into your calling because you think you're not able. You think you don't have the ability, or you're not qualified to do it. Truth is you're not able or capable or qualified, but the grace of God is sufficient for you. In fact, if you have a call that you can do on your own, it's not of God.

LET'S PRAY:

Oh Lord, I think You for your grace. I lift up those who while reading this feel that they are not sufficient. They have bought into the lie that their weakness is what disqualifies them. They do not understand that it is their weakness that qualifies them in the Kingdom of God.

I pray that they will see that in their weakness You are strong; in their weakness Your power is made perfect. That in their weakness, You work best. I pray we would all be like Paul when he said that he would boast all the more in his weakness because he knew that in his weakness, his Lord is made perfect. Let us know that when we are strong, then we are really weak. I lift them up before You, Lord, into Your perfect presence. In Jesus' name, amen!

SUMMARY POINTS

1. Knowing Jesus releases sustaining grace.
2. Weakness becomes the doorway to God's power.
3. Grace is active divine influence.
4. Intimacy with Christ reshapes identity and purpose.

BIBLE VERSES IN THIS CHAPTER:

John 17:1-5
2 Corinthians 12:8-10
Hebrews 4:16
1 Peter 5:10
Luke 4:18

REFLECTION QUESTIONS

1. How has knowing Jesus benefitted you?
2. Do you desire to know Jesus more deeply?
3. Have your thoughts on grace changed after reading this chapter? If so, how?
4. Make a list of things you now can see in your life because you know Jesus.
5. How has grace changed your life?

ADDITIONAL STUDY

Knowing Jesus does not remove weakness from our lives—it redefines it. Many men assume that intimacy with Christ should eliminate struggle, but Scripture teaches the opposite. When we truly know Jesus, we learn to rely on His grace rather than our strength. Weakness becomes the place where God's power rests, not where faith fails.

This chapter challenged the lie that maturity means independence. In God's kingdom, maturity means dependence. The more we know Jesus, the more we recognize our need for Him every single day.

1.
PAUL'S THORN
2 CORINTHIANS 12:7-10

God did not remove Paul's weakness—He revealed its purpose. Grace did not eliminate the thorn; it supplied the power to endure. Knowing Jesus means trusting Him even when relief does not come.

2.
JOHN 15:1-11

Fruit is the result of abiding, not striving. When we disconnect from Jesus, productivity may continue for a season, but life will eventually dry up.

3.
ISAIAH 40:31

Those who wait on the Lord exchange their strength for His. Knowing Jesus teaches us where real strength comes from.

CHAPTER 8

WHAT DOES SURRENDER LOOK LIKE?

Then Jesus went with them to a place called Gethsemane, and he said to his disciples, "Sit here, while I go over there and pray." And taking with him Peter and the two sons of Zebedee, he began to be sorrowful and troubled. Then he said to them, "My soul is very sorrowful, even to death; remain here, and watch with me." And going a little farther he fell on his face and prayed, saying, "*My Father, if it be possible, let this cup pass from me; nevertheless, not as I will, but as you will.*"

– Matthew 26:36-39, emphasis added

So when Pilate saw that he was gaining nothing, but rather that a riot was beginning, he took water and washed his hands before the crowd, saying, "I am innocent of this man's blood; see to it yourselves." And all the people answered, "His blood be on us and on our children!" Then he released for them Barabbas, and having scourged Jesus, delivered him to be crucified.

Then the soldiers of the governor took Jesus into the

governor's headquarters, and they gathered the whole battalion before him. And they stripped him and put a scarlet robe on him, and twisting together a crown of thorns, they put it on his head and put a reed in his right hand. *And kneeling before him, they mocked him, saying, "Hail, King of the Jews!"* And they spit on him and took the reed and struck him on the head. And when they had mocked him, they stripped him of the robe and put his own clothes on him and led him away to crucify him. *As they went out, they found a man of Cyrene, Simon by name. They compelled this man to carry his cross.*

And when they came to a place called Golgotha (which means Place of a Skull), they offered him wine to drink, mixed with gall, but when he tasted it, he would not drink it. And when they had crucified him, they divided his garments among them by casting lots. *Then they sat down and kept watch over him there. And over his head they put the charge against him, which read, "This is Jesus, the King of the Jews." Then two robbers were crucified with him, one on the right and one on the left. And those who passed by derided him, wagging their heads and saying,* "You who would destroy the temple and rebuild it in three days, save yourself! If you are the Son of God, come down from the cross." So also the chief priests, with the scribes and elders, mocked him, saying, "He saved others; he cannot save himself. He is the King of

Israel; let him come down now from the cross, and we will believe in him. *He trusts in God; let God deliver him now, if he desires him. For he said, 'I am the Son of God.'" And the robbers who were crucified with him also reviled him in the same way. Now from the sixth hour there was darkness over all the land until the ninth hour. And about the ninth hour* Jesus cried out with a loud voice, saying, "Eli, Eli, lema sabachthani?" that is, "My God, my God, why have you forsaken me?" *And some of the bystanders, hearing it, said, "This man is calling Elijah." And one of them at once ran and took a sponge, filled it with sour wine, and put it on a reed and gave it to him to drink. But the others said, "Wait, let us see whether Elijah will come to save him."* And Jesus cried out again with a loud voice and yielded up his spirit – Matthew 27:24-50, emphasis added.

Can I ask you what does your surrender look like? Our Lord and Savior asks us to surrender to him. He wants our complete surrender in which we are holding nothing back. I believe that surrender and commitment go hand and hand.

Can we look at what happened on the cross of Jesus Christ in a slightly different way? Can we look at what true surrender looks like? Because I would imagine that if we look at what we call surrender and compare it to what we see in that instance, it would not come close in comparison.

Here is the problem we will have when we see Jesus face to face. We will not be able to say, "You asked me to do things You did not do." Because everything that Jesus is asking us to do, He has done. What does your surrender look like? Is it a daily surrender? Is it a moment-by-moment surrender? Is it a partial surrender? Because anything short of total surrender will not be accepted. We see that Jesus totally surrendered to His Father and to His process. Can I briefly write about those two things? Because if we read between the lines of surrender, we will see how Jesus was completely committed to His Father and to His process.

In order for us to totally surrender to the Lord, we will have to surrender to Him and surrender to the process.

1. Surrendering to the Father

"My Father, if it be possible, let this cup pass from me; nevertheless, not as I will, but as you will."

We must first surrender to the Father. We must say like Jesus, "Not my will be done but your will be done in my life." In order for someone to surrender their will to someone else, they have to be committed to the cause or person to which they are surrendering. This is clear in Jesus' surrender to His Father in heaven.

What does it mean to surrender the will? The will can be described as the desire, wish, purpose, inclination, mind, disposition, intention, or intent of someone. *So, when you surrender your will as Jesus did, you are surrendering your wishes, purpose, mind, and intentions. This says a lot about what surrender requires and looks like.* There is no way we can come remotely close to this if we are not committed to Jesus.

Our surrender starts when we surrender all that we have to our Father in heaven. This is what it means to love your God with all your heart, soul, and mind. It becomes a natural surrender when you love Him in this way. It is impossible to do the will of the Father unless you love Him in this way. Jesus loved His Father with all His heart, soul, and mind.

I can look back at my walk and say that there were times in my life and maybe even times recently when I did not love God our father in this way. I loved Him and I believed in Him but I was not totally sold out for Him. *It is possible to love God and believe in God and not be totally sold out, not be surrendered to Him in every way.*

As we can see here, it began before Gethsemane when Jesus made the pilgrimage to Jerusalem and then again in the Garden when He prayed to see if it was possible for His cup of suffering to pass. As we read the gospel accounts, we see a minute-by-minute act of surrender by Jesus. He knew what He had to do and continued to surrender His will to the Father: "Not my will but your will be done." That is powerful!

We do not know what is going to happen after we say that so we don't say it. Jesus knew that He would be beaten and hung on a cross. Yet He still surrendered to His Father. Can we understand the struggle when Jesus was in the garden praying?

I think we often look at surrender in the wrong way. We look at it like in the movies where we surrender, and it means defeat. It means we lose everything or give everything over to our enemy. We associate surrender with fighting an enemy. But Jesus is not our enemy. When we surrender to Jesus, we do not lose everything but gain everything. When Jesus surrendered unto His Father, what happened next? *The Father placed everything under His feet. Surrender is not the act of losing everything, but the act of gaining it.*

We often miss this point because we do not look at surrender in the right way. What's more, there is another way that we misunderstand surrender. Usually when someone surrenders, they surrender to their enemy and then expect to be treated poorly and unfairly. But when we surrender to Jesus, we are surrendering to the One who created us. We are surrendering to the One who loves us, to the One who has our best interests in mind.

We are not giving ourselves into the hands of someone who wants to mistreat us, but rather into the hands of the One who created us and wants nothing but the best for us. **This** puts a whole new spin on what surrender and commitment look like.

So, the first step in surrender is to surrender to the Father!

2. Surrendering to the Process

And as Jesus was going up to Jerusalem, he took the twelve disciples aside, and on the way, he said to them, "See, we are going up to Jerusalem. And the Son of Man will be delivered over to the chief priests and scribes, and they will condemn him to death and deliver him over to the Gentiles to be mocked and flogged and crucified, and he will be raised on the third day" (Matthew 20:17-19).

We see another two acts of surrender in this passage. We see that Jesus had to surrender to His Father, and Jesus had to surrender to the process. What does it mean that we must surrender to the process? Jesus was totally surrendered to the process that He had to go through. We see here that He was going to Jerusalem knowing that He would be crucified there, but He went anyway.

Jesus knew His purpose in life and surrendered to it. That is both powerful and encouraging. Jesus knew what He was going to go through, yet He did it. Our Father in Heaven knows what you will go through yet He keeps it secret, so you do not have to go through what Jesus went through. This also shows how committed our

Heavenly Father is to us and how committed we should be to Him in return.

We all have a call a purpose under heaven and we must surrender to it. We must surrender to the process that is required to make us sons or daughters of God. If we are not completely surrendered to the process of Jesus, then we are merely practicing a form of godliness and denying the power of God.

When I was not totally sold out to the process of God, I was a fraud. I believed in God but I was not willing to surrender to the process He wanted to carry out in my life. I believed in Him but did not let Him change me. *Is it possible that you can be totally surrendered to the Father, but deny His power to change your life?*

Truth is, I do not believe that you can love God in the way He desires and not let Him change your life. So then, we are green lighting ourselves if we think we can love God and not let Him change us. We must surrender to the process and the call of God.

We see that Jesus totally surrendered to His Father and to the process. Jesus knew that He was born to suffer. Jesus died so we would have salvation and grace, and mercy would be given.

Scripture says, "And Jesus cried out again with a loud voice and yielded up his spirit." The word *yielded* means to relinquish or surrender, which means even in death Jesus had to surrender His Spirit.

We must surrender to our process and calling. Jesus did and He expects us to do so as well. Jesus surrendered to all that He had to do and go through. We must be willing to do the same and this will take commitment. What is amazing about the passage above is that we see Jesus surrendering for the second time.

The first time Jesus was in the garden and praying, "Not my will, but Your will be done." There Jesus was surrendering His will to the Father. Jesus was saying to the Father that the Father's plan was a good plan. We struggle with that because we think our plan is better than God's plan for our lives. But we see clearly that Jesus said, "Not my plan, Father, but Your plan for my life."

How many times have you decided that your plan was better? How did that work out for you? God's plan is always better than your plan so when you surrender to His will, you are surrendering to the better plan.

Then we see Jesus's surrender again at the cross. Here we see that Jesus surrendered His Spirit. Jesus knew that the Scriptures had to be fulfilled, and He had to die on the cross. So, He surrendered His Spirit unto God. What is powerful about this is that Jesus said beforehand that no one was taking His life, but He was surrendering it of His own accord.

If we are honest with each other, we can

see many areas in our lives that we surrender and are committed to. We are committed fans to our sports teams. We are committed to our politics, and we are committed to our hobbies. I love to cook BBQ. Give me a nice day and the smoke is going over some ribs or brisket. I have to be committed to the brisket because it takes hours and hours to cook. But I am willing to stand there and wait for it. So why don't we commit to Jesus in the same way? This will take a surrender much like what we see here with Jesus.

Let me end the chapter with this:

> I have been crucified with Christ. It is no longer I who live, but Christ who lives in me. And the life I now live in the flesh I live by faith in the Son of God, who loved me and gave himself for me (Galatians 2:20).

I love this vers, because Paul says it all right there. When we surrender the way Christ has, we no longer live our own lives, but we live Jesus. It's not that I live and added Jesus, but I live Jesus (read that again). *He died for me, so why shouldn't I live for Him?* Let's truly surrender to Jesus and not to our interests. *The problem we have is that we have been surrendering some things, when Jesus wants us to surrender our lives.* He did it for us. Now we must live for Him.

Jesus wants to live in and through you. *We must stop surrendering stuff and start surrendering us.*

This is a great opportunity here as we go into prayer. It is at the *altar* that God can *alter* us. If you're reading and you want to surrender your life to Jesus, come to the *a-l-t-a-r* and let God *a-l-t-e-r* you. Surrender to Jesus and surrender to the process.

LET'S PRAY:

Lord we come to You as sons looking to surrender ourselves to You. Lord, we say not our will, but Your will be done in our lives. Lord, if we have some mixed up ideas on surrender, please show us the right way. We wish to be like our Savior Jesus as He surrendered to You in Gethsemane. Lord, let our lives be a light that shines for You with lives committed to You in every way. Please do what You will in our lives. We pray this in the mighty name of Jesus!

SUMMARY POINTS

1. Commitment requires presence and consistency.
2. God uses relationships to refine character.
3. Withdrawal is rooted in fear, not strength.
4. Sacrifice sustains healthy relationships.

BIBLE VERSES USED IN THIS CHAPTER :

Matthew 26:36-39
Matthew 27:24-50
Galatians 2:20

REFLECTION QUESTIONS

1. Has your look on surrender changed? How?
2. Can you see a clear process in surrender?
3. How does surrender connect with commitment?
4. Can you be committed and not be surrendered?
5. Is it possible to love God in the way He wants and not be surrendered to Him?

ADDITIONAL STUDY

Relationships are where commitment is tested most clearly. It is easy to talk about loyalty and love in theory, but relationships expose our fears, selfishness, and desire for control. If we are going to keep it real, the way we treat people reveals whether commitment has taken root in our hearts or whether it is still just a concept.

God never intended relationships to be convenient. He uses them to refine us, stretch us, and teach us how to love the way He loves. Commitment in relationships requires presence, patience, and sacrifice—especially when it would be easier to withdraw. When men refuse commitment in relationships, people get hurt. When men step up, lives are protected and restored.

1.
JOSEPH AND MARY
MATTHEW 1:18-25

Joseph could have protected himself, but instead he protected Mary. Commitment cost him reputation and comfort, but obedience mattered more than public opinion. This is what manhood looks like when commitment outweighs fear.

2.
RUTH AND NAOMI
RUTH 1:16-17

Ruth's commitment was not driven by obligation but by love. She chose faithfulness when walking away would have been understandable. Real commitment does not abandon people when circumstances change.

3.
EPHESIANS 5:25

Christ's love defines commitment in every relationship. Love that sacrifices, stays, and gives its love that reflects Jesus.

CHAPTER 9

SHOWING UP!

Let love be genuine. Abhor what is evil; hold fast to what is good. Love one another with brotherly affection. Outdo one another in showing honor. Do not be slothful in zeal, be fervent in spirit, serve the Lord. Rejoice in hope, be patient in tribulation, be constant in prayer. Contribute to the needs of the saints and seek to show hospitality.
– Romans 12:9-13

Eighty percent of success is showing up.
– Woody Allen

Woody Allen was right: you just being there is a start. But can I take you deeper in this idea of showing up? I believe that showing up is closely related to commitment.

I have been doing men's ministry for almost 20 years. I have seen many brothers fall off the path. We have let the world and all it brings distract us at every turn. Because of the world, we are always half in and half out of God's grace and plans.

Recently, we started a new year with the

men's group at Rally Point Church where I pastor. I started a series called 'Show Up.' I challenged the men to be present not just in body, but in spirit—and in heart and in mind.

Have you ever been to a NFL football game? When I go to the game, most times we tailgate. We cook food and have fun joking and laughing as we get ready for the game. When we get to the game, we are focused to pull for our favorite team. We are all there, heart, soul, and mind.

We must take the example of the football game all the more as we pursue our calling in Jesus Christ. Our motto needs to be framed in terms of the questions, Are you here? Have you showed up? That's because many of us have become complacent in our walk and purpose. When that happens, we fall short of what is needed to show up and be committed. Can I challenge you as you read? Can I ask you to go deeper this year and to start showing up? Let's be all in. Let's be committed!

> O Lord, who shall sojourn in your tent? Who shall dwell on your holy hill? He who walks blamelessly and doe what is right and speaks truth in his heart; who does not slander with his tongue and does no evil to his neighbor, nor takes up a reproach against his friend; in whose eyes a vile person is despised, but who honors those who fear the

> Lord; who swears to his own hurt and does not change; who does not put out his money at interest and does not take a bribe against the innocent. He who does these things shall never be moved (Psalm 15:1-5).

David lays it all out there in this plasm. According to him, this is what showing up looks like.

What does it mean to show up? Do you truly love Jesus? Do you truly love God? I am not talking about a worldly love. I am talking about an agape love, a **true love, an honoring love**, and **a dutiful love**. Being able to show up has everything to do with how much you love God, and how much you're willing to let Him love you.

1. A True Love

Let love be genuine. Abhor what is evil; hold fast to what is good. Love one another with brotherly affection (Romans 12:9-10).

Showing up starts with how we treat each other. This passage says to let your love be genuine. That means let's stop with the false fronts and facades. We are called to love each other. The first step to showing up is being genuine with each other in love. Did not Jesus say they will know you are my disciples by your love for each other?

This passage from Romans says to abhor what is evil. So often we see things that are evil and make no attempt to address or stop it. Sometimes we actually partner with it. But in order for us to show up consistently, we must abhor evil in whatever form it takes.

Our Lord and Savior abhors evil. He came into the world to save us from all evil, no matter how slight or egregious it is. Sometimes we see evil and we think to ourselves "Well, it is not hurting me or my family," and we stand by and do nothing. The only way for evil to succeed is for good men to do nothing. Can I challenge you today to go deeper this year? Can we start showing up?

In order for us to abhor evil, we have to care about the things going on around us. If we love our brothers with a genuine love no matter their color, creed, or affiliation, we will see the evil. We will also be able to show up for God and our families.

Before I really got serious about my walk with Jesus, I let so many things pass by and never said or spoke a word. It took me allowing the heart of God to come into my life before I could see what He sees—before I could get mad at the things He gets angry with.

This passage goes on to say hold fast to what is good and to love one another with brotherly affection. This is what it means to show up. When we show up with all our hearts and minds, we hold on to what is good and we love one another with brotherly love.

Do you have any brothers? I have four brothers, and they are all bigger than I am. We would fight from time to time, but God help you if you said or did something to one of my brothers. That is brotherly love. We may have disagreements but when it comes to the love of my brother, I advise you not to mess with them. We are brothers and I won't let anyone mess with them because I love them.

I regularly tell people at services to look at their brother and say, "I won't let anyone mess with you!"

We have to start showing up.

2. An Honoring Love

Outdo one another in showing honor
(Romans 12:10).

Part of showing up is not being only self-aware, but being also aware of others and their needs. This is something we do not do as much as we should—honor one another that is. When I say honor, I mean in love. Perhaps we say things sometimes to flatter people for our own means and gains. But when we honor them out of love, it is genuine and sincere. It comes across in a way that gives God glory.

As we look at it today, we regularly see men from other churches in my Rally Point meetings having fellowship together. There is no competition or animosity, and this is the way it should be. God did not create the church to have its members compete against each other. We are all called to different things, but I see a lot of worldly ways in how we relate. At times, we get to a place where we think we are the only ones who can do it right and thus we look down on everyone else. But just look around at your next church service or men's meeting and remind yourself that we are all brothers of the same Father.

It takes humility to honor others. Honoring each other is biblical. When we do this, we are building up the Body in brotherly love and we are showing the world that we are disciples of Jesus Christ.

This is how we show up, by honoring each other with love. It doesn't have to be an elaborate, formal thing. It can just be as simple as, "Hey brother, it is really good to see you today." It can be a call when we have not seen or heard from a brother.

You know what warms my heart? It is when I am away for a service and I get a call from one of my brothers telling me that I was missed. Then when I come back, several brothers approach me, saying that I was missed. To me, that's honoring me with love.

They took the time to notice that I was not there, and my not being there was felt. Do you know how many guys never come back simply because they feel as if no cares? A simple call or some kind words saying they were missed goes a long way.

This is how we show up!

3. A Dutiful Love

Do not be slothful in zeal,
be fervent in spirit, serve the Lord.

There is a lot said here. So often I see many brothers just who are out of it—there is no other way to put it. There is no fire or zeal in their service to the Lord. Showing up means we do so with all our heart and with enthusiastic zeal. *Zeal* means great energy or enthusiasm in pursuit of a cause or objective.

And with great energy. This means I am pursuing God with all my strength, with all my might, and with great energy. When I come to praise, I come with great zeal because I get a chance to be in the presence of my God. Showing up means coming in excited and with a great expectation to see God move in our lives. We should start getting excited to be in the presence of God. This passage is saying do not be lazy or slothful in serving God. Of all aspects of our lives in which we should be passionate and enthusiastic, it should be serving the Lord.

Be fervent in spirit in serving the Lord. Fervent means having or displaying a passionate intensity. When we root for our favorite teams, we have passionate intensity. We should have that same intensity when we serve the Lord. This is how we show up. This is not just when we feel good or when the mood strikes us or things are going well, but all the time. If you notice it says to be fervent in spirit and serve the Lord! This means that in my deepest places, not just in my outward appearances, I will serve the Lord with a passionate intensity.

That is showing up.

If you have not figured it out yet, I am a pretty intense guy. My desire is to show up in every way and in everything I do, hoping that my passion and strengths glorify my Lord. If you want to glorify our Lord and Savior, then you need to start showing up.

4. In Prayer

Rejoice in hope, be patient in tribulation,
be constant in prayer.

You have the hope of salvation in you. The word of God says that the rain will fall on all. That means we will go through tribulation. But when we show up serving the Lord with all our hearts, we become overcomers. One of the areas that we as men lack in is prayer. This verse says to be constant in prayer. Your heavenly Father wants to hear from you, not just when you're in trouble but all the time.

Can you see how showing up is the brother to commitment? In order to show up in our families, churches, and workplaces, we will have to be committed to our Lord. The Lord is looking for some committed men who will say, "Here I am, Lord"! I don't know about you but that is my cry: "Lord here I am. I will go, Lord. Send me, Lord!" Will you come alongside me?

LET'S PRAY:

If you're reading this and you want to make a declaration to show up, I am going to ask you to repeat after me.

"In the presence of God I promise to show up in all that You call me to. I give You my heart and soul. My desire is to be fully present whenever I am in Your presence. I desire to be present in my marriage, profession, and church. Lord, show me the moments when I am not there. Lord, help me to honor my promise to You. I thank and honor You in Jesus' name, amen."

SUMMARY POINTS

1. Adversity reveals the depth of commitment.
2. Trials refine faith and resolve.
3. Hardship deepens dependence on God.
4. Perseverance produces maturity.

BIBLE VERSES USED IN THIS CHAPTER:

Romans 12:9-13
Psalm 15:1-5

REFLECTION QUESTIONS

1. How do you evaluate your time with Jesus? Are you showing up or are you just there?
2. What would you have to do to show up better?
3. Have you ever thought of what it means to honor your brother? What does it look like for you?
4. In this next year, what can you do practically to show up better?

ADDITIONAL STUDY

Adversity has a way of stripping away surface-level faith. When life is comfortable, commitment is easy to claim. When pressure comes, what we truly believe is exposed. Trials do not create commitment—they reveal it.

This chapter forced us to confront whether our faith is rooted in convenience or conviction. God does not waste adversity. He uses it to refine our dependence on Him and to form perseverance in us. Commitment that survives hardship becomes unshakable.

1.
JOB
JOB 1-2

Job lost everything that gave him stability, yet he refused to curse God. He trusted God without answers. That kind of commitment is forged, not faked.

2.
DANIEL IN THE LIONS' DEN
DANIEL 6

Daniel's commitment did not waver when obedience became dangerous. He prayed as he always had, trusting God with the outcome. Commitment that bends under pressure is not commitment at all.

3.
JAMES 1:2-4

Endurance produces maturity. God uses trials to shape men who can stand firm when others collapse.

CHAPTER 10

LET YOUR YES BE YES! (DON'T BE WISHY-WASHY)

"Again, you have heard that it was said to those of old, 'You shall not swear falsely, but shall perform your oaths to the Lord.' But I say to you, do not swear at all: neither by heaven, for it is God's throne; nor by the earth, for it is His footstool; nor by Jerusalem, for it is the city of the great King. Nor shall you swear by your head, because you cannot make one hair white or black. But let your 'Yes' be 'Yes,' and you're 'No,' 'No.' For whatever is more than these is from the evil one."

– Matthew 5:33-37

How many of us have made oaths that we did not keep?

In days of old people would swear by heaven or earth. Some would even swear by Jerusalem. This is the reason Jesus told the disciples that not one stone would be left on top of another. When we swear by something we are making an oath before God. In some cases, we are even putting that thing before God. We have no control over anything by which we swear, not even control over the number of hairs on our head. We cannot determine if it will rain tomorrow or if the sun will shine. Jesus tells His disciples to let their yes be yes and their no be no because the only thing you can control is your word. This is the beginning of integrity.

> *Integrity: the state of being whole and undivided; the quality of being honest and morally upright.*

The question here is why did Jesus find it necessary to say this to His disciples? He did so because He knew the hearts of men. He knew that they were wishy-washy and unable to commit to anything. This was not how we were created to be. We have become emasculated and not the men we were made to be.

So let your yes be yes.

We must become men of our word. We must do what we are meant to do and what we say we will do. In today's world, our word or our oath means nothing. It used to be a time when you could get a loan from a bank just based on your word to repay it.

The Lord is calling His sons to come together, to be the men He has called us to be, men of integrity. We are to be men not blown to and from by every whim of the wind, but men who do what they say and say what they mean.

Let's talk about three reasons why your yes should be yes and your no be no.

1. It establishes trust.

Definition of Trust: Confidence in or reliance on some person or quality.

Again, you have heard that it was said to those of old, 'You shall not swear falsely, but shall perform your oaths to the Lord.'

When a man is a man of his word, it creates trust with those around him. Before a man's word can be trusted, he first must have his trust in something else. Of course that trust must be in God. It involves being men of God and putting our trust in Him. By trusting in God, we are transformed into the creation we were meant to be.

When God transforms a man, it makes it easier for others to want to follow God and trust in that man. We call out to the Lord to do great things in us and through us, but how can God put anything in Your hands if He cannot trust us with something as simple as our word. How can God use a man or woman He can't trust?

If you are wishy-washy with your word, then you will be wishy-washy in the things of God. A double-minded man is unstable in all his ways (see James 3). God has called you to a mighty purpose, but if you're not trustworthy in the little things, how can you be trustworthy in the big things? How can He give you the things He wants to give you?

When you cannot be trusted, it is like sitting on the floor and eating the crumbs when there is a banquet on the table with every delectable treat you can imagine. If you cannot be trusted, then you are not in a position to receive the blessings that God has prepared for you. By being wishy-washy, you miss your blessings.

Theodore Roosevelt said, "The big jobs are given to those who can show that they can master the little ones first." Honoring your yes is a small but important beginning in establishing trust.

Who do you put your trust in? If it is God, then you have put your trust in a reliable source.

2. It creates stability.

"But I say to you, do not swear at all: neither by heaven, for it is God's throne; nor by the earth, for it is His footstool; nor by Jerusalem, for it is the city of the great King. Nor shall you swear by your head, because you cannot make one hair white or black."

When we show that we are men of integrity, we show the world that we are stable. We are stable in our faith, not wavering when a wind of doctrine that blows our way. We men are adept at coming up with convincing reasons why we are not doing what we should do. Some of you can even make it sound spiritual, acting like you are doing the Lord's work. But the Lord will not have you doing work for Him that will make you appear wishy-washy.

A stable man is like the cedar of Lebanon, strong, sturdy, and unmovable. If you cannot keep your word, then that contributes to your instability. If you are unstable, then most likely your household is unstable. Your finances are unstable; your life is unstable. The Lord is looking for stable people who He can leave this earth to. Then He can move in a mighty way.

Have you ever wondered why we don't see any mighty moves of God? Why don't we see mountains move or storms being stilled? I would imagine if we get enough stable trusting men together, God will move in a mighty way. We would see mighty men doing great feats like in the days of old.

The Lord wants to manifest His own might to the world through His mighty men. Stability creates consistency, which is being the same person all the time in every situation. People don't have to wonder which version of you will show up on any given day. When we are stable and consistent, the Lord knows and has confidence that we will do what He sets out for us to do. Can you see how your yes being yes and your no being no can mean so much to God?

> *"Most men either compromise or drop their greatest talents and start running after, what they perceive to be, a more reasonable success, and somewhere in between they end up with a discontented settlement. Safety is*

indeed stability, but it is not progression." - Criss Jami, Killosophy

What I am talking about is not playing it safe. God does not want us to just play it safe. What I am talking about is the stability in character and moral standing. Stability is faith and our love for God and the willingness to follow Him.

3. It creates commitment

Definition of commitment: the trait of sincere and steadfast fixity of purpose "a man of energy and commitment."

But let your 'Yes' be 'Yes,' and your 'No,' 'No.' For whatever is more than these is from the evil one."

When your yes is yes and no is no, you show that you are not afraid of making a commitment, that you will not run from your oath or your promises. When you say you are a man of God, you are speaking the truth in word and deed. It means not changing faces depending on where you are, or who you're with.

When a man is committed to the Lord, a transformation occurs in that man through the presence and power of the Spirit. Commitment is difficult for a man because when we commit to things, there is a chance something better can come up—or we sense there is a possibility of failure. For most men, failure is the one thing that we cannot handle. I think this is why we are so wishy-washy at times. We are afraid we may fail or be inadequate when we give our word, so therefore we don't give it. But if we can't commit to our word, how can we commit to God?

You say you love God, but you can't make it to church on a consistent basis. You say you love God, but you don't read and study your Bible in a consistent manner. You say you love God, but your prayer life is nonexistent.

The Lord is looking for some committed men; He is looking for some Kingdom soldiers, men He can use. This is the reason your yes being yes and your no being no means so much to the Lord.

Once I made the commitment to serve the Lord and honored it, my life changed from bad to good, from death to life.

> *"There's a difference between interest and commitment. When you're interested in doing something, you do it only when circumstance permit. When you're committed to something, you accept no excuses, only results."* – Art Turock

The Lord will not give you a vision or a purpose if He cannot trust you to pursue it. In my experience, many men struggle today in their faith because they cannot stand on their own word. They vacillate back and forth, and the Lord will not bless what He can't trust. Jesus in the Garden of Gethsemane had a moment when

He asked if the cup of suffering could be taken away from Him. But He gave His word to His Father to let the Father's will be done, not His. He made a commitment.

It was twenty years ago that the Lord gave me a vision of the state or condition of men in New England. From what I saw, we had hit an all-time low with our non-committal attitude. We can't commit to our church, we cannot commit to our wives, we cannot commit to our children. That is why the Lord put it on my heart to start Rally Point Men's Ministry to equip men to be the men they are supposed to be—so their yes can be yes, and their no can be no.

Rally Point focused on the Beatitudes and determined to make them the be-attitudes that each man should exhibit. We made virtues out of each Beatitude, which included attributes like humility, compassion, passion, meekness, purity, diplomacy, mercy, and courage. These are all attributes that Jesus displayed, which again shows that He was and is not asking us to do anything He hasn't done. And because He embodies these attributes, He can empower us to have them as well.

He empowers you so you can develop a Christ-like character and from that integrity is formed. And what is the foundation for integrity? If you guessed let your word be your bond—your yes be yes and your no be no—then you would be correct.

The Lord needs people whose yes is yes and whose no is no. Therefore, you must count the cost before you give an answer or make a commitment. Once you give the answer, however, you must let it stand. No excuses. Are you willing to be trustworthy, stable, and committed? Then let your yes be yes and your no be no. Put an end to all the wishy-washy manhood. The Lord is looking for some men who are willing to say, "Here we are, Lord. Have Your way, use me, transform me. Make me into a mighty soldier."

> "In the same way, let your light shine before others, that they may see your good deeds and glorify your Father in heaven" (Mathew 5:16).

Jesus ended His statement by saying if your yes is not yes or your no is not no, then your behavior or attitude is from the evil one. We are at war and something as simple as a broken word or promise can be used against you in battle. This war is not against flesh and blood but against the principalities and evil forces of this world. This is the reason Jesus said it is from the evil one when you don't keep your word.

Letting your yes be yes and your no be no is another way of saying be committed. If you have struggled in this area and want to make a solid commitment to the Lord, let's pray together. I believe that the Lord will answer the prayers of our hearts. Let's pray!

LET'S PRAY:

Lord, we come before You humbly as Your sons. We do not want to be wishy-washy men in our service of You. We want our yes to be yes and our no to be no. We realize that we cannot do this on our own. We need You, Lord, to help us, transform us, and lead us in life.

Lord, I want to see mountains moved in my life. I know if I am a man of integrity that You will move those mountains for me. Jesus, I want to be more fully committed to You and Your ways. I may not have done all that You have told me to do, or done all that I was supposed to do, but do not leave me to myself. I desire the cry of my heart to be, "Here I am, Lord! Here I am, Lord. Let Your will be done in my life." I pray these things in the mighty name of Jesus, amen!

SUMMARY POINTS

1. Commitment is a daily posture.
2. A committed man lives with integrity and purpose.
3. Obedience becomes a lifestyle.
4. Committed men shape future generations.

BIBLE VERSES USED IN THIS CHAPTER:

Matthew 5:33-37
Mathew 5:16

REFLECTION QUESTIONS

1. In what ways have you been wishy-washy in life, especially in your service of God?
2. What steps can you take now to be a man of integrity?
3. Are you willing to say, "Here I am, Lord"?
4. Has your life been stable and consistent in the Lord?

ADDITIONAL STUDY

Commitment is not proven in a single decision—it is revealed over a lifetime. Many men start well, but fewer finish well. God is not only concerned with how we begin; He is deeply invested in how we live and how we endure.

This chapter called us to examine the trajectory of our lives. Are we growing more faithful, more obedient, and more surrendered as time goes on? Or have we settled into comfort and routine? Living as a committed man of God requires daily obedience, humility, and perseverance.

1.
JOSHUA'S FINAL CHARGE
JOSHUA 24:14-15

At the end of his life, Joshua did not soften his message. He reaffirmed his commitment publicly and called others to do the same. Finishing well requires clarity and courage.

2.
CALEB
JOSHUA 14:6-14

Decades after the promise was given, Caleb still trusted God fully. His strength did not come from youth—it came from faithfulness. Commitment that lasts is built over time.

3.
1 CORINTHIANS 15:58

Faithful labor in the Lord is never wasted. God sees what others overlook, and He honors obedience that remains steady and true.

CHAPTER 11

CAN WE KEEP IT REAL?

"Not everyone who says to me, 'Lord, Lord,' will enter the kingdom of heaven, but only the one who does the will of my Father who is in heaven. Many will say to me on that day, 'Lord, Lord, did we not prophesy in your name and in your name drive out demons and, in your name, perform many miracles?' Then I will tell them plainly, 'I never knew you. Away from me, you evildoers!' "Therefore everyone who hears these words of mine and puts them into practice is like a wise man who built his house on the rock. The rain came down, the streams rose, and the winds blew and beat against that house; yet it did not fall, because it had its foundation on the rock. But everyone who hears these words of mine and does not put them into practice is like a foolish man who built his house on sand. The rain came down, the streams rose, and the winds blew and beat against that house, and it fell with a great crash." When Jesus had finished saying these things, the crowds were amazed at his teaching, because he taught as one who had authority, and not as their teachers of the law.

– Matthew 7:21-29

Have you ever had a friend or someone you know who would always say, "I'm keeping it real" only later to find out that they really did not keep it real? My question for you today is can you keep it real—for real!

There are a few things mentioned in the Bible that keep me up at night and this is one of them. That's because the Scripture says that many will say on that day, "Lord, Lord did I not." This indicates that there are many who are doing the work of the Lord but are doing it for the wrong reasons. Either they are doing it for profit, or for fame, or for power. Their reason may be hidden from plain view but are clearly seen by Jesus.

My question for you today is why do you serve Jesus? Your answer to this question will determine your eternity.

Jesus is always looking at our motives behind our actions. We can fool our friends. We can fool our significant others; we can even fool ourselves. But we cannot fool Jesus.

The worst thing that could happen is we get to the final day, and the Lord says, "Be gone, I never knew you." But if we actually look at it, Jesus is always testing us in this area. At least I know that He is always testing me in this area.

When Marissa and I started our Bible study, we wanted to invite some friends who did not know Jesus. The first meeting we had 15 people in attendance. We were on cloud nine. The Lord asked me if I would I do it for two people. I told the Lord I would do it for two. The next month we had two people show up, and we conducted the Bible study like there were 20 in the room. From that point on, we never had less than eight people, most times with attendance in the teens. Jesus wanted to test our hearts to see if we are doing it for Him or for ourselves—to see if we were keeping it real.

We had Thursday services at a church where I once served. The congregation was being served a spiritual steak dinner every Thursday because the pastors who led it did it as if it were a Sunday service no matter the number of people who showed up. If we are doing it for the Lord, then we would do it with quality and excellence no matter how many are impacted or show up. It matters why we do what we do. Can we keep it real?

So my question to you is why do you serve the Lord? You will be tested, and your eternal destiny depends on your answer. If your answer is anything less than your pure love for Jesus, then you are heading in the wrong direction.

The Spirit's anointing you will receive relies on your reasons for doing what you do. Scripture says someone can tell who those are who serve Jesus by their fruit. I believe this to be true. But it sounds like the two Scriptures conflict with each other. How can I exercise demons in Jesus' name and not get into heaven? Isn't that fruit? Let me let you in on a secret: Sometimes God uses the devil to do his work. What's more, sometimes we start off with the right heart but along the way we lose focus and start to trust and rely on other things. Something else captures and captivates our hearts. We stop doing it for the love of Jesus and start doing it for other reasons. If we do this, we will wind up saying, "Lord, Lord, when did we not do this or that for You?"

May I continue to keep it real?

I can remember at the beginning of my service with the state police. I would get awards, and I would thank God. But soon I was working to please the colonel. My focus shifted from pleasing God to pleasing my oversight. So it was like I was going up and down on a seesaw. Whenever I put my focus on Jesus, good things happened, but when I would put my focus on man, bad things happened.

It was not until I paid attention and saw the ups and downs in my career that I chose to serve God and focus on God no matter the accolades I received. If we all look back, I can guarantee we will see the same seesaw effect in our lives.

We all embrace certain behaviors and habits for reasons other than God. But still Jesus comes into our lives at the toughest times to save us from drugs, alcohol, abusive relationships—the list goes on and on. But as we get to know Jesus, our love for Him increases.

Then our focus for why we are here should change. We should start to do what we do out of love for Jesus and the things that He loves. The way we keep it real is to keep reminding ourselves why we do what we do, examining ourselves to make sure we have not shifted our focus and motivation away from Jesus. The anointing will bring you into some places where the applause and accolades will come. But it is in those times when we seek the world's affirmation and approval that our need for acceptance must take a back seat so the glory can be given to Jesus. We must remember that it was He who brought us where we are. It is because of Him that we are in a position to receive applause.

What are three of the areas where Jesus looks to see if we are keeping it real? He looks to see if we are **realistic**, if we have **relationship**, and if we are **responsible**.

1. Jesus looks to see if we are realistic.

"Many will say to me on that day, 'Lord, Lord, did we not prophesy in your name and in your name drive out demons and in your name perform many miracles?'"

Jesus describes people who appear to have great ministries. They not only call Jesus Lord but also achieve spectacular things in Jesus' name. They prophesy, cast out demons, and accomplish deeds of power in the cause of Christ. Some televangelists come to mind—showmen who tell the lame to throw away their crutches for the benefit of the cameras; who sell prayer handkerchiefs for profit; whose television time is dedicated more to raising funds than to ministry; and who exploit vulnerable people for personal profit.

But we should not assume that Jesus means these words only for others. Who is to say that people with modest ministries are exempt? Is it possible that Jesus might reject a person who spends a lifetime in ministry? Is it possible that Jesus might reject a long-time pastor, elder, deacon, choir member, Sunday School teacher, or board chairperson? If so, by what criteria will they be judged? How will Jesus decide whether to accept or reject each of us? The standard is whether our discipleship is genuine or merely a veneer that provides an attractive exterior to an unfaithful life.

The term *keep it real* comes to mind. More than anyone, Jesus wants us to really keep it real. He wants us to be honest in our walk. That is why He said that He hates lukewarm people (see Revelation 3:16). Jesus would rather you be hot or cold but not lukewarm. He actually said He would spit lukewarm people out of His mouth.

When I was in the 82nd Airborne, we

were sent to Saudi Arabia during Desert Storm. Actually, when I was there, it was called a line in the sand. The temperature was 120 degrees, and they had no way to refrigerate the water but they forced us to drink water so we would stay hydrated. The water was warm and not pleasant to drink. Jesus said if we got like that, He would spit us out. He would rather us be cold but He prefers us to be hot for Him. In other words, He wants us to keep it real as we serve Him.

Why do you serve Him? Are you for real or are you faking it? I understand that sometimes we have to fake it until we make it, but that is not referring to the nature of our heart but instead to our steadfastness in difficult or challenging times. We have to have the right heart condition as we hold on until we make it through whatever situation we may be going through.

Being real in our walk means we understand that Jesus died for us on the cross. It is only because of He did that we can be called sons and daughters of God. So everything I have and everything I have achieved are because of Jesus. That is just keeping it real. I challenge you to look back over your life when you did not know Jesus. It was probably a complete mess. For me, I was heading to death. I wasn't any good for anyone or anything. To look at me, however, you would have seen someone who on the outside looked like they had it all together. But truth be told, on the inside I was a mess. Can I keep it real for you?

The way that I keep it real with others and most importantly with Jesus is to continue to give the glory back to Jesus. I constantly remind myself as to why I am here and why I am doing what I am doing. It is all because of Jesus and for Jesus.

We have to be realistic, lest we find ourselves saying "Lord, Lord" when He states that He never knew us because we couldn't be realistic as to who we were and were not.

2. Jesus looks to see if we have a relationship.

Then I will tell them plainly, 'I never knew you. Away from me, you evildoers!'

In the Bible, knowing a person implies relationship—not mere knowledge. In some cases, it implied a sexual relationship. For example, Adam "knew Eve his wife. She conceived and gave birth to Cain" (Genesis 4:1). In other cases, it refers to a relationship between God and humans.

For instance, the Bible speaks of Moses, "whom Yahweh knew face to face" (Deuteronomy 34:10). Therefore, when Jesus declares, "I never knew you," He means that no relationship exists between Him and the person being judged.

Jesus warns that he will disavow any relationship with the *a-nomian*, a word that comes from the Greek word for *law* (*nomos*). The "a" at the beginning reverses the meaning, so *anomian* means "lawless" and refers to someone who rejected the Torah or Law of God as interpreted by Jesus.

There are those like Simon the sorcerer who only want the power that Jesus has but do not want the relationship with Him (see Acts 8:9-24). Think about this for a second. The God we serve could come and enslave all of us to work and do His will, but He does not do that. Instead He desires to enter into an intimate relationship with us.

In fact, I am now a slave to Him but of my own doing because I desire a love relationship with Jesus. That means I fall in love with Him more and more every day. Because I fall more and more in love with Him, I want to do His will. Does it bother you that I claim to be God's slave or servant? Remember, I am keeping it real in this chapter.

There are so many scriptures that show how our God beckons us to relationship. Here are a few.

> John 15:4-5 – "Abide in Me, and I in you. As the branch cannot bear fruit of itself, unless it abides in the vine, neither can you, unless you abide in Me. I am the vine; you *are* the branches. He who abides in Me, and I in him, bears much fruit; for without Me you can do nothing."

> Isaiah 41:10 – "Fear not, for I am with you; be not dismayed, for I am your God; I will strengthen you, I will help you, I will uphold you with my righteous right hand."

> John 3:16 – "For God so loved the world, that he gave his only Son, that whoever believes in him should not perish but have eternal life."

God is beckoning us so we cannot just acknowledge Him but must have a meaningful relationship! Simply put, we establish a relationship with Jesus in the same way we would establish a relationship with other people. We spend time with Him. How do we do that? We spend time with Him in prayer. We spend time with Him in His word. We spend time with Him meditating on His precepts and His ways. We allow Jesus to occupy space in our minds and hearts, just like we do with our wives, husbands, girlfriends, and boyfriends. We do this just like we do with our best friends. That is how we have a relationship with Jesus.

And as we continue our relationship with Him, our love for Him grows, but our stature in Him grows. That's right. As He transforms us and makes us into His image, our stature or reputation with God increases. He can trust us with more assignments. This may sounds like I am insinuating that we lose who we are. But the truth is, we find who we are–the true and authentic you. This is the you that you were created to be. So the relationship with Jesus is not solely for His sake but also for yours.

It's important that we grasp this. If we do not, we will surely hear Jesus say one day, "I never knew you."

One reason why so many people leave the church and walk away from Jesus is because they want to make following Jesus a religion with rules and traditions when Jesus only wants a relationship. When we make it all about religion, we put a heavy yoke on the necks of the people. Jesus said that His yoke is light (see Matthew 11:28-30). That means He only wants you to love Him with all your heart mind and soul. If you do that and love your neighbor, you are keeping the Law and all God's commandments. We have to stop making a relationship with Jesus into a religious thing and start making it a relationship thing.

Can I keep it real for you?

3. Jesus looks to see if we are responsible.

"Therefore, everyone who hears these words of mine and puts them into practice is like a wise man who built his house on the rock. The rain came down, the streams rose, and the winds blew and beat against that house; yet it did not fall, because it had its foundation on the rock."

You have heard the saying that with great anointing or spiritual power comes great responsibility? In our walk with Jesus as we grow and learn and become like Him, we have a greater responsibility.

Jesus said "the man who hears His words and puts them into practice." You are responsible to put what you have learned into practice, which means you have to do what the word of God says. You have to be obedient.

I tell the men in our men's group this almost every Saturday that they can't come and learn what I am teaching them and keep it to themselves. They have to go out and put it to practice and share what they have learned.

You cannot keep what is given to you and store it away. In the kingdom of God, when we give what we have learned away, God will give us more. We grow more by sharing what God has given you. You are responsible for sharing the information.

There are those who hoard the knowledge that God has given them. When we do that, we are like the one who buried his talents or treasure. When the master came back and asked what he did with his talent, the servant said, "I knew you are a shrewd man, so I hid mine. Here is my one talent."

The master said, "You wicked servant" and he took the one treasure away and gave it to someone else who had ten. In other words, we are responsible for the gifts and wisdom that

God gave us. We are supposed to use and share those gifts with the world so that others will get to know Jesus.

Jesus said the man built his house on a rock. The rain came down, and the wind blew but it did not collapse. When we are being responsible with God's word and talents, we are building our house on a rock. We are trusting in Jesus and relying on Him to lead us in our lives.

When I was a trooper standing on duty at the Providence Place Mall during at the 10,000-person protest march, I had a young women come up to me and call out all the names of those who were slain by the police over the years. As I looked at her, I thought she was crazy. But can I keep it real? But as I thought of it, I was implicitly involved in those deaths. You want to know how? As a police officer and Rhode Island State Trooper, I never did anything or took any steps to help alleviate or improve the situation.

Therefore, I decided that I would receive training in the area of implicit bias and started speaking with officers on fair and impartial policing. If I could show one person that what they bring to the call or situation could result in them responding poorly and cause them to change, or to operate in an unbiased way, then I figured I had done something to help. So then the young girl was right, but since then I have stepped up, and I have stepped in.

We do the same when we see Christians doing things that are a bad testimony of God's presence in their lives but we stand by and do or say nothing. In a sense, we then become a part of the problem. We are responsible when we step in and speak love. Can I keep it real?

Christians are not called to be bystanders. However, we have gone into our church buildings and have shut the world out. We are not called to hide from the world but to change the world. Can I keep it real? In order for us to change the world, we have to be out in the world allowing our light to shine. That is being responsible. We have to start looking after each other and searching for the lost. Time is running short; we are running out of time.

Whatever your talent is, it is supposed to bring you to the masses so you can make a difference. Your anointing is most powerful when it is shared with the lost. Peter and John said, "Gold and silver I do not have, but what I have I will give you" (Acts 3:6). Did the man outside the gate know Jesus when Peter healed him? No, he did not but he knew Jesus after Peter healed him. Can I keep it real? Jesus is looking to see if we are responsible!

Let me end this chapter with this:

When Jesus had finished saying these things,

the crowds were amazed at his teaching, because he taught as one who had authority, and not as their teachers of the law.

Jesus was just keeping it real with the people. I hope that in this book I have kept it real. I don't want you to hear, "Be gone from me; I never knew you." Instead, I want you to be able to say, "Lord, Lord, I did this in your name." But we have to make sure we are real in our approach. Let's make sure we are in relationship with Jesus. Also, be responsible because from those who are given much, much is expected. You have been given much, and much is expected of you.

I want to end with this prayer. If you think that you are lacking in any of these areas, I want you to pray with me. If you have taken this walk for granted, pray with me. If you want a deeper more passionate relationship with Jesus, pray with me. If your responsibility is found insufficient, pray with me. Scripture says many will come and say. Don't be so sure but build your house on the rock. Jesus is the rock and Jesus is here; it is not too late yet.

LET'S PRAY:

Lord, let us be men who keep it real with You. If our commitment to You is lacking, keep it real with us and tell us. Lord, we do not want to hear You say, "Be gone from me, I never knew you." Lord, we want to hear, "Well done, good and faithful servant."

If we are burying our talents, show us, Lord, how we may invest them. Our desire is to give you back much more to You with interest. We desire to be men of God with our lights shining.

Lord, we give You all of the credit for our lives. May You receive glory from our lives. Lord, we love You with all our hearts, souls, and strength. Help us to keep it real with You and all that are around us. Let us be men who are committed to You and all that entails. We pray these things in the mighty name of Jesus, amen!

SUMMARY POINTS

1. Jesus is not impressed by activity; He examines the motives behind what we do.
2. It is possible to serve in Jesus' name without truly knowing Him.
3. Keeping it real requires honesty about our hearts, not just our behavior.
4. Genuine commitment is revealed through relationship and responsible obedience.

BIBLE VERSES USED IN THIS CHAPTER:

Matthew 7:21-29
John 15:4-5
Isaiah 41:10
John 3:16

REFLECTION QUESTIONS

1. What does it mean for you to keep it real?
2. Who should you be keeping it real with?
3. Can you see how commitment factors into what we discussed in this chapter?
4. Have you been real in your approach to Jesus?

ADDITIONAL STUDY

If I can be honest, this chapter should sober every reader. Jesus' words in Matthew 7 are not meant to scare us away from Him but to call us closer—to a real, honest, surrendered relationship. Jesus is not looking for perfect performance; He is looking for genuine hearts. He is always testing our motives, not to condemn us, but to expose what is real and what is not. Keeping it real means we stop pretending and start living from a place of love, relationship, and responsibility.

1.
THE PHARISEE AND THE TAX COLLECTOR
LUKE 18:9-14

The Pharisee looked righteous on the outside but trusted in his own goodness. The tax collector came with honesty and humility. Jesus made it clear which man walked away justified. Brother, keeping it real starts with humility before God.

2.
SIMON THE SORCERER
ACTS 8:9-24

Simon wanted the power of God without the heart of God. He followed the miracles but missed the relationship. This is a warning to any of us who are more interested in what Jesus can do for us than who Jesus is.

3.
THE WISE AND FOOLISH BUILDERS
MATTHEW 7:24-27

Both men heard Jesus' words. The difference was obedience. Keeping it real means we don't just hear truth—we live it. Responsibility is revealed in application.

4.
THE PARABLE OF THE TALENTS
MATTHEW 25:14-30

God expects us to steward what He has entrusted to us. When we bury what He gives us, we are not being cautious—we are being unfaithful. Commitment requires action.

CHAPTER 12

CONCLUSION AND FINAL THOUGHTS

Commit your way to the Lord;
trust in him and he will do this.
– Psalm 37:5

"Commitment is what transforms
a promise into reality."
– Abraham Lincoln

Whether you've just become a Christian, recently renewed your promise to follow Christ, or have practiced your faith your entire life, it's always worth reacquainting yourself with the biblical version of commitment. So here's a simple breakdown of what it looks like and what it requires of us.

1. **It's about trusting in God.** The pledge that we make to God is in response to the many promises He has made to us. But in order to truly commit to Him, we have to believe that He will deliver on His promises.

2. **It requires us to love.** The more we love someone, the more committed we tend to be to

them. Our openness to committing to God is encouraged by the deep love that we have for Him in response to the deep love He has for us.

- 1 Kings 6:61 – "And may your hearts be fully committed to the Lord our God, to live by his decrees and obey his commands, as at this time."
- Deuteronomy 6:5 – "Love the Lord your God with all your heart and with all your soul and with all your strength."
- Matthew 22:37-38 – Jesus replied, "'Love the Lord your God with all your heart and with all your soul and with all your mind.' This is the first and greatest commandment."

3. **It means making sacrifices.** Sometimes saying yes to God means that we have to say no to a lot of other things which appeal to us. People can make the mistake of thinking that our faith restricts our freedom, when it actually develops it. Jesus' sacrifice frees us to pursue a relationship with God.

- Matthew 16:24-25 – Then Jesus said to his disciples, "Whoever wants to be my disciple must deny themselves and take up their cross and follow me. For whoever wants to save their life will lose it, but whoever loses their life for me will find it."

- Matthew 10:37 – "Anyone who loves their father or mother more than me is not worthy of me; anyone who loves their son or daughter more than me is not worthy of me."

4. **It requires doing certain things on a regular basis.** We can recognize how dedicated someone is to another person or thing by how much prominence they give it in their lives. Our commitment to God can't be fleeting, it has to be sustained. In other words, it is a lifelong commitment. Our deeds are an essential way of demonstrating our dedication to Him.

- Hebrews 10:25 – Not giving up meeting together, as some are in the habit of doing, but encouraging one another—and all the more as you see the Day approaching.
- Matthew 18:21-22 – Then Peter came to Jesus and asked, "Lord, how many times shall I forgive my brother or sister who sins against me? Up to seven times?" Jesus answered, "I tell you, not seven times, but seventy-seven times."

5. **It involves giving everything we have.** When we commit to God we have to truly surrender. This doesn't just involve giving up our time and turning away from temptation, it also means actively submitting ourselves to Him.

- 1 Corinthians 6:19-20 – Do you not know that your bodies are temples of the Holy Spirit, who is in you, whom you have received from God? You are not your own; you were bought at a price. Therefore, honor God with your bodies.
- Revelation 3:14-22 – "And to the angel of the church in Laodicea write: 'The words of the Amen, the faithful and true witness, the beginning of God's creation. "'I know your works: you are neither cold nor hot. Would that you were either cold or hot! So, because you are lukewarm, and neither hot nor cold, I will spit you out of my mouth. For you say, I am rich, I have prospered, and I need nothing, not realizing that you are wretched, pitiable, poor, blind, and naked. I counsel you to buy from me gold refined by fire, so that you may be rich, and white garments so that you may clothe yourself and the shame of your

> nakedness may not be seen, and salve to anoint your eyes, so that you may see. Those whom I love, I reprove and discipline, so be zealous and repent. Behold, I stand at the door and knock. If anyone hears my voice and opens the door, I will come in to him and eat with him, and he with me. The one who conquers, I will grant him to sit with me on my throne, as I also conquered and sat down with my Father on his throne. He who has an ear, let him hear what the Spirit says to the churches.'"

Jesus tells the church of Laodicea that they are lukewarm. This is the last church of the churches addressed in Revelation, and this is the church that we find ourselves in today. There are too many men who are lukewarm.

We need to wake up and become alive in Jesus. There are so many promises that the Lord gives, but there are also a lot of warnings as to what will happen if we do not wake up. My brother, my heart cries out for you to be awakened. I want to be with you in heaven celebrating our Lord and Savior.

Thank you for coming this far with me. I pray that your commitment to the Lord has increased by reading this book. There is nothing more important than a man's commitment in the Lord. The world and everything created in it are depending on us. The creation is waiting for the sons of God to be revealed. This will not happen until our Father in Heaven has some men who are serious about following Him, men who are committed to their walk and calling.

He needs men who are desperate to complete their destiny in the Lord. My brother, you are loved by your Lord and Savior, Jesus Christ. He is worthy of your devotion and commitment. May you be blessed and may you ever be committed to serve Jesus with greater depth and fervor.

God bless you!

MORE ABOUT THE AUTHOR

WESLEY PENNINGTON

Wesley Pennington grew up in Cranston, Rhode Island in a family of five boys and one girl, in which he is the youngest. He graduated from Cranston High School East and went on to study sociology at Western Connecticut State University. Wesley then became a member of the United States Army. He served a tour in Korea and upon coming back from Korea, he was assigned to the prestigious 82nd Airborne Division. During his time with the 82nd, Wesley was in one of the first groups sent to Operation Desert Storm.

Upon completion of his military commitment, he returned to Rhode Island where he worked for the West Warwick Police Department. After two-and-a-half years, he left there and went to work with the Rhode Island State Police where he has been employed since 1994. As coach of North Smithfield High School, Wesley's team won the 2019 State Championship and he received the 2019 Football Coach of the Year award. He currently serves as the football coach at West Warwick High School. He is also an ordained pastor. Wesley is married to his wife, Marissa, and has two daughters, Ashley and Eliana.

YOU CAN FIND WES'S YOUTUBE CHANNEL AT

www.youtube.com/c/Wes'sManStuff

ON FACEBOOK

Facebook.com/RPmensministry

ON INSTAGRAM

https://www.instagram.com/p/CUuWhLsrQWu/

ON LINKEDIN

Linkedin.com/in/Wesley-pennington-8575a13a/

CONTACT HIM DIRECTLY THROUGH HIS WEBSITE

www.rallypointmensministries.org

OR BY EMAIL

wesley@rallypointconsultingllc.com

OTHER BOOKS BY WESLEY PENNINGTON

ONE MAN

THE LOVE OF THE FATHER:
ABBA'S PLAN TO RESTORE THE FAMILY

THROUGH THE SMOKER:
WHAT BBQ CAN TEACH YOU ABOUT
HOW GOD PREPARES A MAN

www.ingramcontent.com/pod-product-compliance
Lightning Source LLC
LaVergne TN
LVHW010617100826
845148LV00014B/3010

* 9 7 8 1 6 3 3 6 0 3 5 3 0 *